Ayurveda Primer

The A, B, C's of Ayurvedic Medicine

by Swami Sadashiva Tirtha D.Sc.
(Ayurvedic Medicine & Research)

Author of the Amazon #1 bestseller, The Ayurveda Encyclopedia

Copyright © 2000 – 2017 – Swami Sadashiva Tirtha, D. Sc.
Doctor of Science, Ayurvedic Medicine

ISBN13 978-0-9797445-9-4
ISBN10 0-9797445-9-8

All rights reserved. No part of this e-book may be used or reproduced in any way without written consent from the publisher except for brief quotations used in critical articles or reviews.

This book is for educational purposes only. It is not intended to treat, diagnose, or prescribe. For all health concerns persons are advised to consult qualified health practitioners.

Introduction

As health care costs continue to spiral out of control patients, doctors, and insurance companies are all feeling the strain of costly health coverage. The medical notions of the past centuries are crumbling; we need a new medical paradigm if we are to be successful in treating diseases and helping those who cannot afford insurance.

Some drugs seem to be losing their effect. Infectious diseases such as TB that were once considered cured, are now returning. Modern-day diseases are resistant to antibiotics, yet these drugs are contributing to the development of new degenerative diseases. However as medical care becomes less effective, medical costs continue to rise.

Certainly, many new drugs have been developed, helping relieve or cure various diseases. Yet if the past track record of drugs is any indication, these drugs will cause some serious side effects in the future—perhaps even for the next generation. And while prescription drugs help many conditions, they are the fourth leading cause of death in this country (JAMA, April 15, 1998); this is 2 1/2 times more deaths than due to AIDS. Clearly with all the benefits allopathic medicine offers, the costs, side effects and lack of ability to heal have reached a level that demands better solutions. It is the patients—the people who have led the country's interest in alternative or holistic medicine, with more than 40% of Americans trying some form of alternative health care (JAMA, May 20, 1998). Further, they have chosen to pay for these treatments out of their own pockets rather than use their pre-paid health insurance.

Doctors and pharmacists report their patients are asking about alternative care. As a result, doctors, pharmacists and health insurance companies are educating themselves in alternative methods. Pharmaceutical companies are now developing herbal products, doctors are becoming licensed in acupuncture and insurance companies are beginning to cover certain alternative therapies.

This book discusses the world's original or oldest medicine, Ayurveda, as a solution to the problems of the modern health care system—offering cost-effective, safe, and quick healing.

Western medicine already recognizes India as the country that first practiced rhinoplasty. What may not be realized is that India's original medical system, Ayurveda, was also the first to perform artificial limb replacement and other surgeries more than 2,000 years ago.

Along with surgical practices, alternative therapies were heavily relied upon; herbology, nutrition, aromatherapy, hatha yoga, meditation, and the like. In fact, surgery was only used in emergencies, while other therapies were practiced as the first line of healing, prevention, and longevity.

Ironically, the world's oldest medical system is now proving to be the best answer to solving the problems of medicine for modern times. This book will discuss

Ayurvedic theory, as well as case studies and scientific research that shows Ayurvedic health care is more cost-effective, safe and quick healing than allopathic medicine.

The purpose of this book is to show patients, doctors, and health insurance companies that there is strong, replicable proof that Ayurvedic health care can make modern health care less expensive, safe, and effective in healing diseases. It is this author's hope that in some way this information can help improve the quality of health and healthcare for the people of today and into the 21st century.

Swami Sadashiva Tirtha February 1999; Bayville, NY, USA

I've made a few upgrades to this book since 1999, updating the research studies, adding photos, and a few minor changes. Previously this book was only available to my Ayurveda certification students, and now thanks to new publishing technology, I am able to release it to everyone.

While my Ayurveda Encyclopedia is a great reference book on all things Ayurveda, this Ayurveda Primer gives quick tips at a glance.

I hope this book is helpful for everyone looking for mind-body-spirit healing, prevention, and rejuvenation. At this time in our lives we as a planet are beginning to realize on a larger scale, that compassion and joy are the best mind-body-spirit medicine. The rest are adjuncts to the expansion of our inner light

Swami Sadashiva Tirtha February 2017; Unadilla, NY, USA

Dedication

This book is dedicated to my guru, His Holiness 108 Sri Sri Srimat Swami Narayan Tirthaji Maharaj who guides all aspects of my life—now from the afterlife more than ever.

To all people everywhere in need of compassion, joy, and wellness

Table of Contents

Introduction..ii
Dedication..iv
Table of Contents...v

Section 1: What Is Ayurveda?...................................1
Chapter 1: Introduction..2
Chapter 2: Tridosha Theory;
    Ayurvedic fundamentals.. ………......17
Chapter 3: Analysis & Disease
    Development….....…………..………37

Section 2: Therapies..51
Chapter 4: Herbs..52
Chapter 5: Food..65
Chapter 6: Massage, Yoga, Exercise
    and Sleep……………………….105
Chapter 7: Mental Therapies meditation, music,
    aromas, color……………….....115
Chapter 8: Pancha Karma……..………....130

Chapter 9: External Considerations: Climate /season, buildings, Jyotish- Vedic astrology......................136

Section 3: Illustrations & Validations............................152
Chapter 10: Case Studies....................................153
    Pet therapy research..........173
Chapter 11: Research................179
Chapter 12: Frequently Asked Questions.......................213

Afterword..............................241
Glossary..................................250
Self-Education.........................257
About the Author.....................258
Bibliography...........................263
Index......................................274

Section 1 What is Ayurveda?

Chapter 1 Introduction

Why Alternative or Holistic Medicine?

News item: More than 40% of Americans with health insurance are opting to pay out of their own pocket to visit holistic health counselors instead of receive free Western medical care under their health insurance plan.

News item: HMO's are now considering covering alternative medicine for their members.

News item: The ninth leading cause of death in the US is death due to prescription drugs. Drugs are responsible for more deaths than AIDS.

An awareness in America is emerging. People are dissatisfied with medical care as we know it. Costs are too high, medicines cause side effects, and doctors have no answers for many diseases. Simultaneously, people are discovering inexpensive, effective holistic or natural therapies to heal simple, chronic, and serious diseases. People are finding they are able to take more control of their lives and their health.

What is Alternative or Holistic Medicine?

Alternative medicines are natural therapies that offer an alternative to modern Western or allopathic medicine. Holistic has several meanings. First it means viewing the whole life of a person. Each area of life affects the other areas (i.e., mind, body, career, relationships, exercise and spirituality). For example, stress at work may be causing headaches or high blood pressure. So, in addition to treating the symptoms with natural therapies, the holistic approach would look to help reduce the stress at work through lifestyle changes.

All sectors of life are viewed as different areas of the same web of life. If one area is shaken, the whole web shakes. When considering the symptoms of a disease, the holistic practitioner looks at the root causes of the disorder. Is the person getting enough rest and proper nutrition? Are they exercising? How is their social or family life? Are they happy in their career? Are they spending some time pursuing their spirituality (however each person defines spirituality)?

So, holistic means looking at the whole person. It also means considering spirituality as the foundation of all areas of life. The holistic viewpoint often finds that when a spiritual crisis or emptiness exists, all areas of life suffer, including one's health.

Actually, alternative or holistic medicine may be properly called complimentary medicine as it compliments modern Western medicine. Western medicine, in many cases, offers superior diagnostic and therapeutic approaches. However, it has become clear to the public as well as the medical profession that allopathic medicine does not have all the answers. Further, doctors have not been trained in preventative care—the foundations of holistic medicine.

Holistic medicine compliments modern medicine by offering:

1) The knowledge of prevention 2) The ability to heal diseases without side effects. 3) An assessment of the root cause of disease. 4) Healing methods for diseases such as asthma, arthritis, cancer, etc. where modern medicine has no answers.

What is Ayurvedic Medicine?

Ayurveda (pronounced *I-your-vay-da*) is the first or oldest healing science, dating back more than 5,000 years.

All forms of natural and modern medicine can trace their roots to Ayurveda. Nutrition, herbology, surgery, gynecology, artificial limb replacement, acupuncture, massage, yoga, aromatherapy, meditation, etc. all were written about by the ancient Ayurvedic doctors.

Yet the most important aspect of Ayurveda has been retained only in this system of healing—the personalization of treatment. It recognizes that people have different constitutions that need to be considered when applying therapies.

Ayurveda offers therapies to heal disorders that are presently considered incurable by modern Western medicine, such as arthritis, asthma, cancer, and some forms of diabetes.

Therapies include herbology, nutrition, yoga, meditation, aromatherapy, exercise, music therapy, color therapy, lifestyle and spiritual counseling.

To summarize, Ayurveda offers a unique alternative medicine approach for four main reasons

1) It looks at the fundamental or root cause of illness; it does not merely treat symptoms.

2) It offers personalized or tailor-made therapy suggestions.

3) The results are gentle, effective healing with no side effects.

4) Ayurveda takes a holistic view of the client, looking at mental and physical health, career, relationships, possible environmental causes and spiritual life.

Development of Ayurveda

Around 1,500 BC Ayurveda developed eight specialized branches of learning.

1) Internal medicine 2) Ear, Nose & Throat 3) Toxicology 4. Pediatrics &

midwifery 5) Surgery 6) Psychiatry 7) Aphrodisiacs 8) Rejuvenation (longevity or age reversal).

Advanced Civilization

The ancient Ayurvedic doctors, as well as other Vedic specialists from other professions possessed amazing knowledge, without the use of modern microscopes and telescopes. In the first century AD, a major text on Ayurveda, the *Charak Samhita*, gave a detailed description of the development of a fetus in each of the nine months of pregnancy. The description is almost exactly identical to currently known stages of development found with modern technology. Ancient astronomers cited the distance from the earth to other planets. These distances are within a few inches of what has been verified by today's high powered telescopes.

Another astonishing insight is Ayurveda's understanding of six stages of disease development. Only the last two stages can be detected by modern technology. It is clear that this ancient culture possessed a wisdom unknown today.

Spreading of Ayurveda

India was at the center of the Silk Road, the major trade route between Europe and Asian countries. At the center of the Silk Road was a famous Ayurvedic university, *Nalanda*. Travelers from Greece, Tibet, Middle East and Europe came to study Ayurveda and bring this information back to their homelands.

Decline and Re-emergence of Ayurveda

Over the millennium, various countries, religions and cultures attacked India. Each new conqueror closed down various aspects of Ayurveda—colleges, surgical practice, etc. Still Ayurveda remained intact in the haven of the Himalayan Mountains and in Southern India where conquerors did not go.

In 1920, the Indian government began restoring Ayurvedic knowledge by rebuilding universities and colleges. Now over 150 Ayurvedic universities and 100 Ayurvedic colleges exist. Many more educational facilities are being planned.

Definition of Health

Ayurveda defines health as a state of dynamic equilibrium or balance. When all aspects of one's life (nutrition, career, exercise, relationship, environmental and spirituality) are in balance, health exists. If even one area of life is out of balance, one's health begins to suffer. The greater the imbalance, the more concrete the health problem.

Many factors can affect one's balance— foods, spices, job satisfaction, climate, season, travel, emotions, sleep patterns, exercise, etc., achieving balance becomes an on- going process. Like the person surfing on the ocean, trying to maintain balance, people become `health surfers' aiming for equilibrium each day and season.

While this initially may sound complicated, Ayurveda offers a few simple guidelines to monitor all that influences one's state of balance. If a person feels a little 'off' one day, it is the first sign of imbalance. By simply taking proper herbs, foods, exercise, etc., balance is quickly restored and a potentially more serious illness is averted.

The Goal of Life

Ayurveda says the goal of life is to achieve Self- Realization or spiritual enlightenment. The purpose of Ayurveda is to resolve the mental and physical health disorders that are obstacles on the path. A balanced life translates into physical health and mental peace. Only the peaceful mind can begin to realize its true nature.

This true nature is said to be the state of eternal Divinity. When a person realizes that they are not the body or their thoughts but are in fact the eternal soul, they are said to be Self-Realized. In the ancient Ayurvedic text the *Charak Samhita*, it is said that the first cause of illness is the loss of faith in the Divine.

A Self-realized person sees all of life as a part of their unbounded, eternal nature, much like a drop of water in the ocean sees itself and all water drops not as individual fragments, but as the ocean. This is the definition of faith in the Divine; it is faith based upon the actual experience. So, loss of faith in the Divine means a loss of this experience.

One begins to see objects as separate from themselves. One's unbounded eternal nature becomes veiled. Seeing an object as separate from oneself creates a longing or desire to have that object in the attempt of feeling full or eternal. But the reality of unbounded eternity is that the object is already a part of the person; they just don't realize it.

By following one's personalized Ayurvedic suggestions, the mind begins to return to a more peaceful or clear state. Through meditation one can regain the experience of the one-ness of all of life.

Summary

This chapter has defined Ayurveda as a holistic or all-inclusive science where all areas of life need balance to experience optimal health. This is achieved through a personalized, gentle, effective method without side effects and costly treatment.

Ayurveda addresses the root cause of illness, rather than treating only the symptoms. It offers new insights into health and balance that give modern health care new options, complimenting modern Western medicine in four areas of life:

1) Mental and physical health
2) Meaningful career
3) Meaningful relationships
4) Meaningful spiritual development

The goal of Ayurveda is to achieve balance or health and remove the blocks towards complete mental peace or Self- Realization.

Chapter 2 Ayurvedic Theory

Many people feel that understanding health is an issue beyond their grasp. Ayurveda offers a simple, nurturing theory that is understandable even for children.

Fundamentals of Health

Ayurveda asks the question, is there something that is common to all aspects of life—people, foods, climates, disease, emotions etc.? We know from physics that all people, animals, objects, and nature are made up of common elements. All these different manifestations contain molecules, atoms, sub-atomic particles, etc. A chair is different from a human, but they are the same in that they are both made up of atoms. So, what is the most fundamental level common to all things?

Ayurveda says that the foundation of all of life (animate and inanimate) are the five elements—ether, air, fire, water, and earth. These elements are actually energies, and not actual fire, air, etc. Everything in life has various combinations of these elements. Lighter objects contain more ether and air. Denser objects contain more water and earth.

These elements combine in different ways to produce different types of people, animals, and objects in nature. For example, a thin person can be said to have more ether and air. A hot-tempered person can be said to contain more of the fire element. A heavy-set person would contain more water and earth. From this viewpoint, we can begin to see how people have individual or personalized constitutions.

Disease and the Elements

In the same way, each disease can be seen as containing 9 excesses of one or more of the elements. The nature of ether and air is dry, cold, and wind or movement. Disorders that contain these symptoms include dry skin, gas, brittle bones, or cold extremities. A person with these symptoms can be said to have ether (space) and air excesses; they have too much of these elements and not enough of the fire, water, and earth elements.

The nature of fire is heat and moisture. Disorders whose symptoms include heat include hot temper, acid indigestion, fever, sweating, and inflammation. A person with these symptoms is said to exhibit fire excesses with deficiencies of ether, air, water and earth.

Water, weight or mass, and cold are all aspects of the water, and earth nature. Disorders that exhibit excess water and earth include phlegm or mucus, sinus congestion, lung congestion, overweight and edema. These symptoms are attributed to a person with excess water and earth elements.

More serious diseases can also be identified according to their symptoms. A person whose arthritis is aggravated by cold weather or putting their hands under cold water are said to have too much ether/air or exhibit an ether/air form of arthritis. The person whose arthritis is aggravated by hot weather or placing their hands in hot water, and has inflamed joints exhibits a fire form of arthritis. The water form of arthritis is revealed by swollen joints with pockets of fluid, which becomes aggravated during damp or rainy weather.

An excess of one, two, or even all three of the elemental groups (ether/air, fire, or water/earth) can cause many diseases. From this insight, Ayurveda is able to offer more specific therapies that focus on each specific type of arthritis.

Herbs, Foods and The Elements

Just as people and diseases are element-predominant, so too are foods and herbs. Onions, garlic, and chili are fire predominant foods and spices. Broccoli, golden seal, and bitter melon are ether/air predominant. Sweet fruits, sweets, and zucchini are water/earth predominant.

Achieving Balance

So far, we have discussed the elements in people, diseases, and foods and spices. Let us integrate these conditions to see how Ayurveda achieves balance in a person with disease.

Let us return to the example of arthritis. We have three people, each with a different elemental excess. First is the ether/air-excessed person. Cold and dry symptoms are already in excess. We said in Chapter 1 that health means balance. To achieve balance in the case of ether/air- excessed arthritis, a person needs to avoid exposure to these elements in their food and herbs to prevent further exacerbation of the situation. Simultaneously they need to build up the deficient elements, fire, water, and earth.

Thus, they need to avoid foods and spices that increase ether and air such as golden seal and bitter melon. Balance will be gained by eating moist and hot foods and spices like sweet fruits, zucchini, black pepper, and ginger.

Ether/Air Excess

Water/Earth + Fire **Deficiency** Deficiency

The above diagram illustrates a scale with three balance cups. The person with ether/air-excessed arthritis has their corresponding scale cup too high. Their fire

and

water/earth cups are too low. We can say in this example that this person needs to put more fire, water, and earth elements in their ether/air cup to bring the cup down. This will automatically raise the other two cups to a level of balance between the three cups.

This approach gives insight not only into how Ayurveda achieves balance or health, but also reveals why generic treatment of a disease can cause side effects. If a certain food or herb reduces arthritis but its primary element is ether/air, it will increase the air in some other part of the body, possibly causing gas, constipation, dry skin or bones, or perhaps a more serious condition.

Three types of the herb exemplify personalized herbal treatment, *guggul* are helpful for arthritis. *Yogaraj guggul* (warm and moist properties) is best for the ether/air form of arthritis. Fire-caused arthritis is healed with *Kaishore guggul* (cooler properties). Pure *guggul* (warm and dry properties) is best for water/earth-caused arthritis.

So Ayurveda diagnoses a disease by looking at its elemental excess. It heals the disease by applying therapies that nourish or supplement the deficient elements. In this way, balance for this person and their condition is attained.

The Elements and Personal Constitutions

Ayurveda analyzes a person's life-long physical constitution as well as the current constitution based on their health concern. Generally, ether/air constitution people develop ether/air disorders because these elements naturally tend toward excess.

In some cases, a person can develop a disease related to elements different from their constitution. For example, an ether/air constitution person can develop a cold with abundant clear or white mucus. The cold is a water/ether- excessed condition. With the knowledge of the person's constitution and the elemental excesses of the disorder, Ayurveda aims to offer therapies that balance the condition (the cold) without aggravating the physical constitution. In this case, warm herbs such as ginger and pepper heal the cold because warm foods balance ether/air and water/earth. Ether/air is warmed and water/earth is loosened and dried by heat. Thus, Ayurvedic insights offer a gentle healing approach without causing side effects to the person while healing the disorder.

The personal constitution is called *dosha* in Ayurveda. The life-long constitution or nature of the person is called *prakrti*. A current health condition is called *vikrti*. Ayurveda groups the five elements into three main constitutions or *doshas*, Vata is the name given for the ether/air *dosha*. Pitta is the name given to the fire *dosha*. The water/earth *dosha* is called Kapha.

The balanced or healthy Vata *dosha* is energetic, adaptable, and creative. When excess Vata exists, these people can develop brittle bones, dry skin, gas, constipation, worry, fear, and anxiety.

Balanced Pitta *doshas* are leaders, goal-oriented, warm, and athletic. When Pitta becomes excessed these people can develop infections, inflammations, rashes or acne, hot temper, impatience, liver, gall bladder, or spleen disorders.

Healthy Kapha *doshas* are loyal, calm, and nurturing. When excess Kapha occurs, they can develop edema, excess weight, respiratory disorders, become lazy, possessive, and greedy.

No one *dosha* is preferred or better than another. What is important is to know one's *dosha* to keep it balanced. Medically speaking *doshas* are related to humors. Vata *dosha* is associated with wind, Pitta with bile and Kapha with phlegm. Thus, all disorders related to each of these humors can be traced to its corresponding *dosha*.

Generally, people are not a pure, single

dosha. Seven *dosha* categories exist, 1) Pure Vata 2) Pure Pitta 3) Pure Kapha 4) Combined Vata/Pitta 5) Combined Vata/Kapha 6) Combined Pitta/Kapha 7) Combined Vata/Pitta/Kapha (called *tridosha* or all three *doshas*).

When treating dual *doshas*, the third *dosha* is used to achieve balance. For example, in a Vata/Pitta *dosha*, Kapha therapies are used for balance or healing. In the case of the *tridoshic* person herbs and foods that do not aggravate any of the *doshas* are used. However, in many diseases it is not possible to find *tridoshic* herbs and foods. In this case, the *dosha* causing the most problems is treated first until its symptoms subside and another *dosha* causes the predominant aggravating symptoms. Healing *tridoshic* diseases is the most difficult of the conditions.

Taste: Foods & Herbs

To better understand why foods and herbs have elemental properties we need to discuss what is called the "energetics' of taste. Ayurveda says a total of six tastes exist—sweet, sour, salty, pungent, bitter, and astringent. Each taste relates to different elements. Sweet tastes (sugar or starches) have the properties of moistness and coolness. When a person has a cold and eats sweets more mucus develops; the sweet taste produces more moistness.

Thus, sweet tastes contain the elements of *Kapha* or earth and water. Therefore, they are beneficial for the Vata and Pitta *doshas* because these constitutions have a tendency towards excess ether/air and deficient water. Sweet tastes restore the balance to Vata or Pitta individuals. [It is important to note that when considering actual sweets (e.g., cake, candy) Ayurveda refers to whole cane sugar products such as the product 'Sucanat' or maple syrup.

White sugar has all the nutrition removed from it so nourishment cannot be derived from it. This is why eating white sugar harms the body. The body works to digest the sugar but in the end, gets no nutrition from its efforts. It is like working an eight-hour day and only to have the boss tell you they aren't going to pay you. Eating white sugar detracts more than it offers.

Sour foods, such as fermented foods or acids, contain the elements of earth and fire. The Pitta or fire person would be aggravated by such tastes (e.g., lemon, lime or grapefruit) because they add even more heat to an already excessed fire constitution. Sour is better for Kapha *dosha* because the heat dries the water. Vata *doshas* may also receive some benefits from sour tastes because the fire warms the cold air while the earth grounds them.

Salty tastes (salt and alkaline) contain the elements water and fire. Only the Vata *dosha* is benefited from this taste. Salt adds water retention for the Kapha *dosha* and heats the Pitta constitution.

Pungent tastes (spices, acrids, and aromatics) comprise fire and air elements. Thus, they are best for Kapha *doshas*. Ether and air are contained in bitter tastes, making them ideal to balance Pitta and Kapha *doshas* while aggravating the Vata individual. This is why broccoli, a slightly bitter vegetable causes excess ether/air in Vata *doshas*, thus producing gas. Astringent tastes (tannin-constricting quality) contain earth and air elements, most suited for the Pitta *dosha*. The earth element may aggravate Kapha *doshas*.

Many other forms of *dosha* and illness detection are available. Discussed here are some of the diagnosis techniques that are widely used. A consultation with an Ayurvedic practitioner often involves a discussion of symptoms as well. The client's description of their symptoms also reveals which *doshas* are imbalanced. Words like hot tempered, cold circulation, etc. clearly indicate the elements involved in the health concern.

See the *dosha* self-test on next page. You may take the dosha self-test by answering the questions according to your entire life—not just your current situation. Further, you may check more than one category if you feel you fit into two or three classifications

BODY	Vata	Pitta	Kapha
Body frame	thin	medium	large
Finger nails	thin or cracking	medium, pink, soft	thick or white
Pulse	80-100	70-80	60-70
Weight	low or bony	medium, muscular	gains easily
Stool-move bowels	small, hard, gas	loose or burns	moderate or solid
Forehead size	small	medium	large
Appetite	variable	strong or sharp	constant or low
Eyes	small or unsteady	reddish or piercing	white or wide
Voice	low or weak	high or sharp	deep or tonal
Lips	thin or dry	medium or soft	large or smooth
Chest	flat, sunken	moderate	round, expanded
Nature (which bothers you most)	cold and dry	heat and sun	cold and damp
Chin	thin or angular	tapered	round, double chin
Neck	thin or tall	medium	big, wide, folded
Body Totals			

MIND	Vata	Pitta	Kapha
Memory	quick to grasp ideas-soon forgets	sharp or clear	slow to learn- but never forgets
Beliefs	radical, changing	leader, goal oriented	constant or loyal
Dreams	flying or anxious	in color or fighting	romantic or few
Speech	quick or talkative	moderate or argues	slow or silent
Finances	spends on trifles	spends on luxury	saves money
Sleep	light	moderate	heavy
Habits	travel or nature	sports or politics	water or flowers
Mind	quick or adaptable	penetrating, critical	slow or lethargic
Emotions	enthusiastic or worries	warm, can get angry	calm or attached
Temperament	nervous or fearful	impatient	easy going
Mind Totals			

Dosha Self-Test Copyright © 1998-2017 Swami Sadashiva Tirtha. Reprinted with permission from Ayurveda Encyclopedia

Summary

This chapter discussed the Ayurvedic diagnostic methods. The root cause of illness and its development is found by looking at both subtle and manifest symptoms. Illness begins in the origin sites of the *doshas*—the stomach, small intestine and colon for Kapha, Pitta and Vata respectively.

Determination of one's *dosha* and current imbalance (*vikrti*) are learned through observation, self-tests, and questioning the client. The diagnostic tools are simple yet highly effective in quickly and accurately pinpointing one's *dosha* and the elemental cause or causes of a disorder.

Once the *dosha* and elemental cause of disorders are learned, therapies are applied to heal conditions without causing imbalance or side effects. The various therapies are discussed in Section 2.

Chapter 3 Analysis & Disease Development

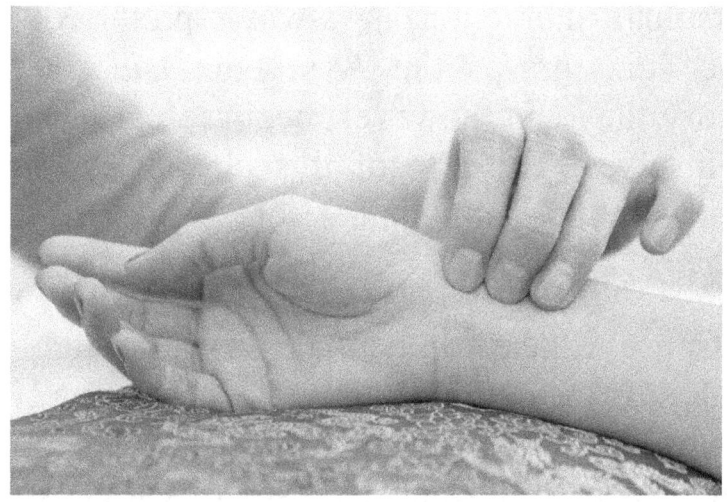

With a little training, most people can learn to monitor their own state of health and determine what elements are causing their illness as well as what foods, lifestyle, mental or spiritual conditions have created the imbalance.

While this book aims to offer a simple explanation of Ayurvedic self-care, it is always best to initially receive a complete consultation from a trained Ayurveda practitioner; books can only teach so much. Personal interaction is always preferred. Once one grasps the Ayurvedic *tridosha* theory they can, however, begin to care for themselves. The aim of this chapter is to explain the simplicity of Ayurvedic diagnosis.

1) Cause: Illness can be understood through analyzing the cause (i.e., When did it begin? What was different at that time? What was eaten? Was there some extra stresses at work or home? Did the weather or season have any effect on the condition?).

2) Hidden signs: What are the subtle indications felt to indicate an imbalance has begun? Can they be related to any of the elements?

3) Symptoms: Once an illness is clearly

evident, which of the elements are predominant?

4) Observations: What other signs are observable? The face, nails, stool, urine, skin, pulse, all give clues to which organs and elements are imbalanced.

The Three Origin Sites of Illness

With the exception of externally-caused disorders such as broken bones, or burns, all internal disorders begin in one of three organs. Kapha excesses begin in the stomach. The small intestine is where Pitta excess starts. Vata excesses originate in the colon. By keeping these three areas healthy and balanced, disease has no chance to develop. Once a *dosha* is in excess in one of these organs, they spread to other areas of the body. The developmental pattern of disease follows below.

Understanding the Subtle Symptoms

A common story is heard from family and friends. 'I went to the doctor but they couldn't find anything wrong with me. They said it was my imagination'. Modern Western diagnosis, whether using human or technological measurement, is not able to see the earliest stages of disease when only a subtle imbalance exists. However human intuition is readily able to note when something is wrong—even if it is minor. Thus, prevention of disease is possible. Ayurveda says six stages of disease development exist. Modern medicine can only detect the disease in the last two stages, when illness has already become serious.

1) Accumulation: This is the earliest stage of imbalance. Mild symptoms can occur or persons just feel a little out of balance. A *dosha* or *doshas* are becoming slightly excessed. For example, a slight excess of Kapha may cause one to feel lethargic. Accumulation takes place in one of the three *dosha* origin sites (i.e., stomach, small intestine or colon).

2) Aggravation: As the *doshas* begin to become more excessed they begin to aggravate some condition such as cough or mucus. Aggravation is still confined to one of the three origin sites.

3) Overflow: When the origin organs have filled up with the excess *dosha*, the excesses have nowhere to go but to overflow into the plasma and blood, moving to the gastrointestinal tract. Symptoms begin to grow worse. In the Kapha example, a person may find himself or herself easily winded.

4) Relocation: The overflowing *dosha* excesses will begin to collect somewhere in the body that is weak or susceptible. The lungs, being close to the stomach are an easy target for Kapha excess to relocate. Breathing may become more difficult at this stage, but still easy to heal.

Modern medical technology would still not notice any health condition at this stage.

5) Manifestation: The excessed *doshas*, having relocated and developed, begin to be noticed due to quantity or mass. At this point Western medicine is able to detect a clinical disorder. In our Kapha example the person would be diagnosed with asthma. Healing is still possible but takes longer to achieve.

6) Distinction, Chronic and Complication: This final stage occurs when a disorder is left untreated. Not only is the disorder more serious, but chronic and secondary

complications can occur at this advanced level.

With the knowledge of the four early, subtle levels of imbalance, Ayurveda validates people's intuition that something is wrong. Further, therapies are available to easily correct the imbalance at these early stages, preventing more serious diseases from occurring.

Observation

We have discussed the relationship between elements and foods. Other relationships exist to help determine the elemental cause of disease and the organs affected. The face can reveal disorders of all three *doshas*. Worry lines or dry skin indicate Vata mental or physical excesses respectively. Rings under the eyes indicate kidney disorders. Vertical wrinkle lines just above and in between the eyebrows show Pitta disorders (the left of center line shows spleen excesses; the right of center line shows repressed anger and liver excesses).

Thin, dry, or cracked lips, and/or a coating on the back or the tongue indicate Vata excesses. When the middle of the tongue is coated or painful pimples appear, Pitta is in excess. A coating on the front third of the tongue indicates Kapha toxins. When the tongue coating is white, undigested food toxins (*ama*) is present in the body. Should the coating turn yellow or green, infection has set in.

A crack down the middle of the tongue reveals either spine or immune system weakness. Teeth mark indentations around the front arc of the tongue indicate malabsorption due to excess Pitta [in this case the digestive fire is too high and not only digests the food but burns up the vitamins and minerals; no nutrition is left to be assimilated to nourish the body.

Yellow or green mucus also indicates infection or inflammation somewhere in the body (a Pitta excess). Abundant white or clear mucus indicates excess Kapha exists. White spots on the finger nails indicate zinc or calcium malabsorption.

Another important Ayurvedic diagnostic tool is a special type of pulse analysis. This pulse-taking approach offers information regarding a person's *dosha* and current health condition (*vikrti*). *Dosha* pulses are taken before 10:00 a.m. when a person is seated and rested. Ideally it is taken first thing in the morning after visiting the bathroom and before eating or any physical exertion. After 10:00 a.m. only the current health balance can be learned.

The *prakrti* or *vikrti* is learned by feeling the wrist under the index, middle, and ring finger. If the pulse if felt under the pointer, Vata predominates. When the middle finger first feels a pulse, Pitta is dominant. Kapha is most influential when the pulse is felt under the ring finger.

The pulse rate also can indicate a person's *dosha*. A person with a pulse rate of 60-70 beats per minute is a Kapha *dosha*. A Pitta *dosha* pulse is between 70-80. The Vata *dosha* pulse is between 80-100.

A subtler pulse reading involves the quality of the pulse. The Vata pulse will feel quick, thready, irregular, possibly skipping a beat every so often. It will feel like the movement of a snake. A strong, bounding, consistent pulse is a Pitta pulse. This pulse will feel more like a hopping frog. The Kapha pulse is warm, slow, consistent and feels like a swan, gracefully beating. Of course, for the person with a combination of two or three *doshas*, two or all three pulses will be felt.

Advanced pulse taking can also reveal the health of the organs, tissues, and emotional and spiritual life. Pulse analysis is not a process easily learned and is best performed by a trained Ayurvedic practitioner.

Another useful method to determine the *dosha* is the 'self-test'. Below is a sample questionnaire to determine one's physical and mental *dosha*. To take this self-test, circle the words that are most descriptive over one's entire life (i.e., not just over the last weeks or months). If two or all three categories describe the person, all three categories can be marked. The totals are added at the bottom. Physical and mental totals are separated to better identify the different *doshas*. In this way treatment can be more specific.

Many other forms of *dosha* and illness detection are available. Discussed here are some of the diagnosis techniques that are widely used. A consultation with an Ayurvedic practitioner often involves a discussion of symptoms as well. The client's description of their symptoms also reveals which *doshas* are imbalanced. Words like hot tempered, cold circulation, etc., clearly indicate the elements involved in the health concern.

Summary

This chapter discussed the Ayurvedic diagnostic methods. The root cause of illness and its development is found by looking at both subtle and manifest symptoms. Illness begins in the origin sites of the *doshas*—the stomach, small intestine and colon for Kapha, Pitta and Vata respectively.

Determination of one's *dosha* and current imbalance (*vikrti*) are learned through observation, self-tests, and questioning the client. The diagnostic tools are simple yet highly effective in quickly and accurately pinpointing one's *dosha* and the elemental cause or causes of a disorder.

Next therapies are applied to heal conditions without causing imbalance or side effects. The various therapies are discussed in the following section.

Section 2 Therapies

Chapter 4 Herbs

Herbs are perhaps Ayurveda's most effective method in restoring health and offering prevention and longevity. Herbs work in two ways—herbs that work on specific organs and herbs that have a specific therapeutic action. Examples of herbs that are specific to organ or tissue healing are herbs that work on the brain, liver, and eyes. Examples of herbs with a specific action or characteristic are laxatives, nervines, and antimicrobials.

While herbs play a large role in healing, prevention, and longevity, it is better not to think of them as the 'magic pill' that will cure all diseases even if one maintains unhealthy eating, working, relationship, and spiritual habits. Herbs always work best when used in a holistic manner; when herbs are used in conjunction with therapies for other areas of one's life (e.g., nutrition, exercise, lifestyle, spirituality) a quicker and more permanent state of healing occurs.

Below are a list of the best herbs for organs and health concerns. Usually main herbs are mixed with secondary herbs in more complex formulas. For the purpose of simplicity only the main herbs will be listed.

Best Herbs for Organs

Adrenals- gotu kola

Blood- manjishtha, turmeric

Brain- gotu kola

Colon- triphala

Eyes- triphala

Female reproductive- shatavari

Heart- arjuna

Immune system- shatavari, ashwagandha

Kidney- shilajit, punarnava, gokshura

Liver- bhumyamalaki (for Pitta or Kapha *doshas*) bhringaraj, gotu kola, punarnava (for Vata *doshas*)

Lungs- vasak

Lymph- kaishore guggul, jasmine (for Pitta or Kapha) – bayberry for Vata

Male reproductive- ashwagandha

Mouth- triphala

Muscle building- ashwagandha

Nerves- gotu kola, ashwagandha,

Pancreas- gurmar (removes sugar from pancreas)

Skin- manjishtha, turmeric

Spleen- punarnava, kutki

Tendons/ligaments- turmeric

Veins- manjishtha (cleanse and circulate blood)

Best Herbs for Specific Disorders

Acid indigestion - fennel seeds

Acne - manjishtha Allergies - follow *dosha* diet and take digestive herbs Anemia - chyavan prash, turmeric, ghee, saffron, punarnava in boiled milk, iron ash (loh bhasma-but not for sickle cell anemia)

Anger - gotu kola, rose, sandalwood

Antioxidants - turmeric, chyavan prash, sesame seeds (and green leafed herbs)

Anxiety - gotu kola

Arthritis - yogaraj guggul , kaishore guggul (Pitta), guggul (Kapha)

Arteriosclerosis - yogaraj guggul, turmeric, aloe, safflower, myrrh

Asthma - vasak, vamsha lochana, pippali,

bala, ajwan

Athletes foot - turmeric and guduchi (for infection/tea tree oil for white fungus)

Broken bones- manjishtha

Candida - musta

Chemotherapy strengthening - shatavari

Cholesterol - guggul

Circulation (cold extremities) - turmeric

Colic- fennel

Constipation- triphala

Cough/cold/flu- pippali, ginger, black pepper, vasak, vamsha lochana

Depression- jasmine

Diabetes- gurmar (for pancreas), shilajit (for

kidneys)

Diarrhea/dysentery- ishabgol, triphala

Digestion- cardamom, coriander, fennel

Dysmenorrhea- manjishtha, sesame seeds, red raspberry, myrrh, mint, aloe vera gel

Ear disorders- nirgundi

Eczema- gotu kola, bhringaraj

Epilepsy- gotu kola, pippali

Fear- gotu kola

Fibroids (uterine/ovarian)- ashok

Gall stones- gokshura with coriander, manjishtha

Gas- fennel, cardamom

Hepatitis- manjishtha, bhringaraj, amalaki,

turmeric

High blood pressure- arjuna, gotu kola

Impatience- gotu kola, rose, sandalwood

Impotency- kapikachu (atmagupta)

Jaundice- manjishtha, neem, aloe vera gel, turmeric

Kidney stones- gokshura, manjishtha

Lethargy- gotu kola

Low blood pressure- cloves

Memory- shank pushpi

Menopause- shatavari, manjishtha, musta, saffron, myrrh, aloe vera

Menorrhagia (excess)- manjishtha, haritaki, red raspberry

Menstrual cramps- saffron

Mononucleosis- chyavan prash, jatamanshi

Morning sickness- red raspberry

Nausea- red raspberry

Pain (muscle, arthritis, bone, etc.)- mahanarayan oil (external use)

Parasites - kutaj/guduchi immune

PMS- musta

Psoriasis- gotu kola, manjishtha, barberry

Senility- shank pushpi, gotu kola, ashwagandha

Sprue- kutaj, bilwa, ginger

Stress- gotu kola

Toothache- 3 drops of clove oil on tooth

Tumors- manjishtha (malignant or benign), guggul, aloe vera gel

Ulcers (intestinal)- shatavari, licorice

Urinary bladder stones- gokshura, manjishtha

Urinary tract infections- gokshura

Weight- garcinia, triphala, tulsi, ginger (for Kapha *doshas*. Pitta *doshas* can take if balanced with cooler herbs)

Worry- gotu kola

Yeast Infections- musta

Precautions

* No laxatives are taken during pregnancy
* Hot spices are avoided by Pitta *doshas* (e.g., garlic, onion, chili)
* Dry, bitter astringent tastes are avoided by Vata *doshas* (e.g., potato chips/dry, golden seal, raspberries/astringent)
* Sweet, moist tastes are avoided by Kapha (e.g., milk, maple syrup)
* Use saffron in small doses

Herb Doses

At my center I found that herbs are very effective even in small quantities. The following guidelines are based upon our experience.

* 1/4 - 1/2 tsp. 3 times daily for mild to

moderate conditions

* 1/2 - 1 tsp. 3 times daily for strong symptoms

* Larger doses in serious diseases (consult an Ayurvedic practitioner)

* 1/16 - 1/8 tsp. for young children, pets and the elderly

Summary

Generally, herbs have the strongest and quickest healing action on diseases. Herbs can be suggested to work directly on organs and tissues, or to work on specific health conditions such as nervines or antimicrobials. Herbs should be used in conjunction with other lifestyle therapies, and not only as a magic pill to cure a disease.

Chapter 5 Nutrition

After herbs, nutrition is the next most important Ayurvedic therapy. Below are food plans for each *dosha*. When healthy, persons can eat all foods in moderation. When imbalance occurs, the food plans need to be followed more carefully.

General

* Eat fresh, organic foods

* Avoid canned and stale foods

* Cooked whole grains are best

* Eat fruits and vegetables according to season

* Yeast free breads are best (or at least toast bread)

* Mung beans are the only bean that doesn't cause gas

* Avoid eating mutually contradictory foods (see chart on page 53)

* Lassi (yogurt water with cumin seeds is best taken with meals for digestion).

* Ayurveda suggests it is better to gradually reduce animal product consumption except when weak. Animal products are full of steroids, hormones, antibiotics, chemicals, and disease (from sick animals). When

eating animal products, these drugs affect humans, weaken their immune system and possibly causing various mental and physical disorders. Animal products are also difficult to digest, which can lead to a build-up of undigested toxins that is at the cause of all illness.

* Milk is boiled, cooled, then taken with cinnamon or fennel, and cane sugar or honey.

Vata

* Vata *doshas* eat every three to four hours

* Steam vegetables

* Cabbage, broccoli, cauliflower, sprouts cause gas

* Soak dry fruit overnight

Pitta

* Pitta *doshas* eat every four to five hours
* Avoid garlic, onions, and chilies

Kapha
* Kapha *doshas* can skip breakfast

Vata Dosha

Fruit

lemon	strawberries	all berries	baked apple
lime	raspberries	kiwi	baked pear
grapefruit	pineapples	sweet melon	soaked dry fruit
cherries	papayas	rhubarb	peaches
grapes	mango	oranges	plums
apricot	pomegranate	persimmon	banana
avocado	papaya	fresh figs	sweet berries

Vegetables

sweet potato	Seaweed	artichoke
carrots	some avocado	cucumber
beets	green beans	mustard greens
cilantro	fresh peas	fresh
parsley	squash	zucchini
okra	watercress	

Grains

wheat	white basmati rice	oats
khus khus	Brown rice (if digestible)	

Dry grains like granola, chips aggravate the air element.

Beans

Most beans cause gas, are drying and promote constipation except for

mung	aduki

Nuts and Seeds

almonds	sesame seed butter
walnuts	pecans
pine nuts	

Nuts are heavy, nourishing, moistening, and hard to digest and so they are taken in small amounts. Nuts are soaked overnight (almond skin is peeled off before eating).

Oils

sesame oil	ghee
almond oil	avocado oil
butter	

Dairy

boiled milk	ghee
lassi +	unsalted butter
unsalted cottage cheese	home-made cheese (paneer)

+ Lassi Preparation: 1/2 cup yogurt -1/2 cup water, digestive herbs, all mixed and drank at mealtime to aid digestion).

Sweets

cane sugar	jaggery
maple syrup	raw honey
sucanat	demerera

Condiments

rock salt	cardamom
ginger	cloves
cumin	cinnamon
fenugreek	coriander
fennel	basil (tulsi)

Animal Products

Ghee and *lassi* are good meat substitutes (see dairy). Fish and eggs are easily digestible. White chicken and turkey are also not as harmful as red meat and pork.

Beverages

water with lemon or lime and cane sugar	fennel tea
sour fruit juices	mint tea
licorice/ginger tea	gotu kola tea
fruit and vegetables above- taken as juice	

Vata/Pitta Dosha

Fruit

berries	fresh figs
cherries	plums
coconut	pineapples
baked pear	sweet melon
baked apple	some avocado
grapes	mangos
kiwi	oranges
watermelon (chew some seeds if gas appears)	

Vegetables

squash	okra
artichoke	rutabaga
asparagus	zucchini
cucumber	green beans

The cabbage family causes gas, i.e., broccoli, cauliflower, Brussel sprouts. Root vegetables like beets and carrots may be too heating.

Grains

white basmati rice	khus khus
wild rice	wheat
oats	amaranth

Barley is good for reducing fire, but may create gas

for the air aspect of your constitution.

Beans

| mung | garbanzo beans | aduki |

Nuts and Seeds

soaked almonds	sesame tahini
coconut	sunflower seeds

Oils

ghee	sesame	olive (unheated)
sunflower	unsalted butter	

Dairy

boiled milk	*lassi* +
kefir	unsalted cottage cheese
unsalted butter	Homemade cheese

+ *Lassi: 1/2 yogurt -1/2 water, digestive herbs, all mixed and drank at mealtime to aid digestion.*

Sweeteners

jaggery	Sucanat
maple syrup	

Condiments

cardamom	rose water
coriander	vanilla
cumin	mint
fennel	saffron
black pepper	

Animal Products

poached or boiled egg whites	white poultry

Beverages

boiled milk	raspberry tea
chamomile tea	lemon grass tea
fennel tea	licorice tea
fruit and vegetables above, taken as juice	

Vata/Kapha Dosha

Fruit

lemon	berries	cherries
lime	baked apple	peaches
grapefruit	baked pear	apricots

Vegetables

beets	carrots	fresh peas
cilantro	fresh corn	squash
parsley	green beans	artichoke
olives	mustard greens	cucumber

Grains

white basmati rice	barley (if it doesn't cause gas)
monitor all other grains	

Beans

monitor all other grains	monitor all other grains

Nuts and Seeds

3-4 soaked almonds	tahini
Monitor other nuts and seeds	

Oils

sesame	ghee	mustard

Dairy

ghee	lassi +
Monitor milk and homemade cheese	

+ Lassi: 1/4 cup yogurt: 3/4 cup water. Add cumin seeds

Sweeteners

raw honey	cane sugars if they don't cause congestion

Condiments

cardamom	cinnamon
fennel	basil/tulsi
ginger	fenugreek

Animal Products

eggs	white poultry

Beverages

mint tea	fennel tea
fruit & vegetables from the above list	

Pitta Dosha

Fruit

apple	fig
pear	pineapple
pomegranate	mango
cranberry	plum
persimmon	grapes
melon	raspberries
prune	date

Vegetables

cauliflower	cilantro	broccoli
sunflower sprouts	celery	alfalfa sprouts
cabbage	Brussel sprouts	asparagus
lettuce	beans	peas
cucumber	okra	squash

Root vegetables (beets and carrots), nightshades (eggplant, tomato, potato), mustard greens, parsley, spinach, and sweet potatoes may cause difficulty. Hot spicy foods like chilies, garlic, onions, pickles and radishes greatly increase the fire element.

Grains

white basmati rice	blue corn
granola	barley
long grain brown rice	quinoa
oats	millet
khus khus	

Beans

mung	aduki	split peas
lima	kidney	garbanzo

It is advised to coo k beans with cumin or cardamom to aid in their digestion.

Nuts and Seeds

coconut	sunflower

Oils

ghee	sunflower
unsalted butter	

Dairy

ghee	boiled milk
unsalted cottage cheese	lassi +

+ Lassi: 1/2 part organic yogurt: 1/2 part water Add a few drops of rose water

Sweeteners

cane sugar	maple syrup	Sucanat

Animal Products

egg whites	white poultry

Beverages

aloe vera gel	mint tea
boiled milk	apple juice
berry juice	dandelion tea
chamomile tea	burdock tea
vegetable juices from the vegetable list above	

Pitta/Kapha Dosha

Fruit

apple	apricot
pear	dry fruit
pomegranate	raisins

Vegetables

asparagus	broccoli	Brussel sprouts
burdock root	cabbage	fresh corn
cauliflower	celery	green beans
dandelion	collards	lettuce
okra	peas	squash
sprouts	watercress	green peppers

Onions, garlic and chilies aggravate Pitta.

Grains

barley	basmati rice
cooked oat bran	wheat bran (moderation)

Beans

mung	navy
black-eyed	white
aduki	pinto
lima	tur dal
chana dal (garbanzo/chick pea)	

Nuts and Seeds (in moderation)

pumpkin	sunflower

Oils

ghee	sunflower

Ghee (clarified butter) can be taken in moderation (2 tsp./day). Sunflower in moderation.

Dairy

ghee	lassi +

+ Lassi :1 part organic yogurt: 3 parts water

Sweeteners
very little raw honey or cane sugar

Animal Products

poached or boiled egg whites	white poultry

Beverages

aloe vera	apricot	chamomile tea
apple	berry	dandelion tea
pear	barley tea	mint tea
vegetable juice from the list above		

Kapha Dosha

Fruit

Lemon	dry fruit
Lime	apple
grapefruit	cranberry

Vegetables (steamed)

chilies	carrots	asparagus
cabbage	green beans	lettuce
celery	peas (fresh)	cilantro
broccoli	beets	watercress
mustard greens	alfalfa sprouts	sunflower sprouts
chard	cauliflower	spinach

Grains

barley	quinoa
dry or popped grains	corn
millet	rye
buckwheat	basmati rice

Beans

aduki	lima
lentil	split pea
split pea	mung

Nuts and Seeds

pumpkin	sunflower

Oils

mustard	safflower
sunflower	

Dairy

lassi +	goats milk

+Lassi: 1/4 cup organic yogurt: 3/4 cup water. Add cumin seeds and drink with meal to aid digestion.

Sweeteners

small quantities of raw honey

Condiments

dry ginger	turmeric	coriander
mustard	cloves	basil/tulsi
horseradish	cinnamon	cilantro

Animal Products

white poultry

Beverages

dandelion tea	grapefruit juice
boiled goats milk	lemon or lime juice
pineapple juice	celery juice
pomegranate juice	any green vegetable

Mutually Contradictory Foods

Certain food combinations cause immediate imbalance or subtle toxic reactions in the body. Ayurveda says continual use of these combinations leads to skin diseases, blindness, sterility, fainting, anemia, sprue, edema, rhinitis, fever, insanity and in some cases, death. Below are some examples of foods that do not mix well together.

milk and fish	honey and ghee in equal amounts
meat with honey, sugar, milk, or sesame seeds	drinking hot water
milk after radish or garlic	milk with sour items

Summary

There is a strong correlation between nutrition and health. Proper nutrition—according to one's *dosha*— transforms food into medicine, healing and balancing disorders and preventing future diseases.

Chapter 6 Massage, Yoga, Exercise and Sleep

Massage

Ayurvedic massage is called *abhyanga*. It is different than Swedish massage, which relates more to soothing muscle manipulation. The aim of *abhyanga* is to get the oil (usually herbal medicated oil) into the skin.

From here, the oil nourishes all seven tissue layers (plasma, blood, muscle, fat, marrow, bone, and reproductive tissues). The oil also draws toxins from these tissues and brings them to the skin or at least gets them into the blood stream where they can be eliminated later through other Ayurvedic practices.

Abhyanga offers many benefits. * Stimulates and cleanses the lymphatic system * Reverses or prevents aging (i.e., increases longevity) * Improves sleep * Calms and tones the nervous system * Removes mental and physical fatigue and stress * Improves vision * Nourishes and tones the body.

Many forms of *abhyanga* exist. Persons can receive *abhyanga* from one, two, or four practitioners at a time. *Abhyanga* can also be done on oneself. A bottle of sesame oil is placed in a sink of hot water until oil is warmed. Then the oil is applied to the entire body. Focus is given to the feet and anywhere stress accumulates (e.g., neck, shoulders, and lower back).

Massaging one's feet before bed releases stress and promotes sound sleep. This process is recommended to those with insomnia, mental stress, and eye problems. For those with muscle, nerve, or joint pain an herbal medicated oil (*Mahanarayan* oil) is mixed into the sesame oil. The medicated oil removes pain from arthritis, sports injuries, lower back ache, muscle aches, and MS.

Hot-Oil Head Abhyanga

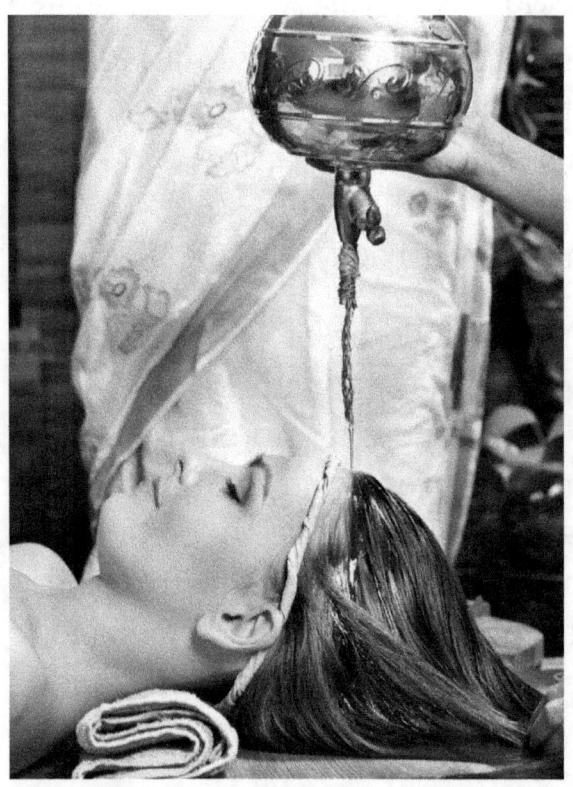

Another popular *abhyanga* technique is a hot-oil head massage (*shiro dhara*). In this therapy, warmed sesame oil is poured in a stream onto the forehead. Clients describe this process as very calming to the mind and body.

All the nerves in the body meet at the third eye, so when the oil massages this area the entire nervous system gets massaged and profoundly relaxed. In this state, deep seated stresses are released. The immune system is also relaxed and strengthened. The mind experiences bliss. Afterwards, clients look and feel 20 years younger.

Ayurveda suggests shiro dhara for all mind and brain disorders (e.g., anxiety, impatience, and tumors, MS) as well as physical diseases like sciatica, tension, and diabetes.

Yoga

Another excellent therapy to reduce mental and physical stress is through yoga postures. Yoga means union. In this case union relates to improving mind-body coordination and developing mental peace. Yoga postures are simple stretching positions that,

* calm the nerves * reduce mental stress * massage and tone muscles * heal various health disorders * stimulate acupuncture

points * develop greater peace of mind * improve memory and concentration * stimulate and balance hormonal fluids

Vata and Pitta *doshas* are more suited for gentle seated and prone postures. Kapha *doshas* do better with standing and more strenuous postures. Yoga classes are inexpensive and are available through many adult education programs, libraries, and from local yoga teachers.

Exercise

Some sort of exercise is important for the integration and well-being of the mind and body. It offers some time away from mental and physical stresses of daily life and work. Walking is the best exercise of all. General advice is to walk at least three times a week for a minimum of 30 minutes.

Vata *doshas* are advised to gently exercise, until they begin to sweat or feel tired. They have the most fragile systems. It is not healthy to put undue stress on their nervous and immune system. Good exercises for Vata include walking, swimming, cross-country skiing, yoga, and tai chi.

Pitta *doshas* can exercise a little longer, but need to drink some liquids before and after working out to prevent over-heating. Recommended exercise for Pittas include walking, swimming, downhill skiing, tai chi, and yoga.

Kapha *doshas* need demanding physical exercise. They have the strongest systems. Also, since Kapha tends towards a sedentary lifestyle exercise helps stimulate and thereby balance them. Jogging, wind surfing, swimming, weight lifting, and walking are some of the better forms of exercise for Kapha *doshas*.

Professional and semi-professional athletes, or for those who are trying to build stamina, the above suggestions have to be modified. However, the general guidelines can still be considered when developing a routine.

Pre- and post-exercise yoga stretches are advised. Yoga before exercising prepares the body by loosening and stretching the muscles, ligaments, and tendons. After exercise yoga helps the body cool down and prevent tightening of the muscles, ligaments, and tendons.

Sleep

Rest is very important for proper rejuvenation and release of stresses. In today's fast paced society people often seem not to receive adequate rest.

Vata *doshas* need the most sleep—around

six to eight hours. It is better for them to retire early and rise early. Pitta *doshas* can do with around six hours of sleep. Early to bed and early to rise is also advised for Pitta *dosha*. Kapha *doshas* actually do better with less sleep—stay up later; get up earlier (without naps during the afternoon).

Summary

We have discussed how massage, yoga, exercise, and sleep are important therapies in improving health and quality of life.

Chapter 7 Mental Therapies

Meditation, Music, Aroma and Color Therapy

Chapters four through six focused on healing through physical therapies. Although these approaches help the mind, they offer mainly physical benefits. (Herbology is an exception; certain herbs target the mind.)

Meditation

We have already discussed the theory behind meditation as well as some common misconceptions. Different meditation styles are discussed below because people relate to different meditation approaches.

Watching One's Breath - 10 Minute Meditation

Purpose: This meditation calms and relaxes. 1. Simply lie on your back on a soft carpet. Feel comfortable, lower the lights, and avoid drafts. 2. Take a deep breath in then exhale. Repeat several times.

a) Feel the inhalation cleansing the body and mind.

b) Feel the exhalation releasing mental stresses, 'shoulds', guilt; and physical tension and toxins out of the body, shoulder, and mind. 3. After three or four breathing cycles the inhalation may actually start to cause the mind to become quieter.

4. Now relax and just watch as your breathing goes on by itself. You don't have to do anything or think about it; it is as if someone else is in charge of your breathing. 5. If thoughts come or go it doesn't matter. Wherever the mind goes is all right.

6. After 10 or more minutes you can get up.

See if you don't feel a little more rested, calmer, and rejuvenated. See how the rest of the day or evening goes after this breathing meditation. *This meditation is especially useful after returning from work.*

Watching One's Thoughts - 10 Minute Meditation

Purpose: This meditation help to understand one's mental patterns. 1. Lie on your back on a soft rug or blanket. 2. Pretend you are in the audience of a play at your local theater only your thoughts are the actors instead of actual people. 3. Treat your stressful thoughts (e.g., anger, impatience, worry, fear, lethargy, etc.) as the villain of the show. Just as you wouldn't jump up on stage and become involved with the actors, do not react to your thoughts; simply observe the thoughts or feelings. 4. Notice any patterns that may create stress for you. 5. Notice if one idea leads to a deeper notion or feeling. 6. After 10 minutes or more you can get up. See if you can be less controlled by your thoughts and feelings afterward the practice. See if you can replace the stressful thought patterns with healthier mental habits.

Talk To God

However, you define the Almighty, talk to God. Here are some suggested approaches.

* Ask to hear what you need to hear. If no answer comes,

* Ask to be ready to hear what you need to learn. (Sometimes persons ask questions but do not want to hear the actual answer; they want to hear another answer. So, they say, 'God doesn't answer me'. The Judeo-

Christian idea of God involves guilt and severe punishment. The Vedic view of God is a more loving, forgiving, and nurturing one. Often guilt-ridden people, afraid that God is cruel and vindictive, may think the answer will come in the form of severe punishment. This is not so.

* Play music, paint, or engage in any hobby that makes you feel a silent connection to the Divine. Let your intuition guide you rather than any judgments whether you are good at what you are doing. It may help to imagine it is God who is playing the music or painting through you; you are only the instrument

Mantra Meditation

Below are five mantras for various situations. They can be mentally recited any time or anywhere. It is best to use the mantras while sitting quietly with eyes closed, but they can be repeated while waking, driving, etc. (with eyes open). The mantras can be recited as long and as often as one wishes.

Shanti- This is the popular mantra for peace of mind.

Ram- (as in calm) Calms the mind from fear and anxiety. This mantra creates a sense of Divine protection.

I'm- This is the education mantra, improving concentration, communication, and intelligence.

Shreem- Is the creative artist's mantra, improving creativity, prosperity, health and harmony.

Som- This mantra boosts the immune system life sap (*ojas*).

Music Therapy

Ayurvedic healing is available through each of the five senses. Herbs and foods heal through the sense of taste. Massage, yoga, and exercise heal through the sense of touch. Meditative music heals through the sense of sound. We will also discuss aromas and colors that heal through the senses of smell and sight respectively. The vibratory effect of mantras heals through all five senses.

'Music soothes the savage beast'. Music also calms the overactive mind. Stores and restaurants, aware of the effects of music, play slow or fast songs to keep people shopping or hurry them out of the store at closing time. Meditation music can include any songs or instrumentals that help one relax. Even recordings of rain, oceans, or waterfalls help calm the mind.

Classical Indian music offers several special

meditational properties beyond general relaxation. The deepest levels of meditation and relaxation are affected. In a book, *The Secret Life of Plants* different music was played for plants. When rock music was played, the plants grew away from the speakers. When classical Western music was played, the plants grew towards the speakers. When Indian *ragas*, as they are called, were played for the plants, the plants wrapped themselves around the speakers.

In a more recent study, three songs were played to 40 heart patients in Berlin. The music included modern music, music by Strauss and *sitar* music by Ravi Shankar. The modern music raised stress levels. Strauss' music lowered stress hormones in the patients. Stress hormones were even lower after listening to the *sitar* music. The *sitar* also reduced the patient's blood pressure.

In addition to the general meditational quality of classical Indian music, *ragas* offer even subtler therapeutic help. Indian musicians know that music played in certain keys relate to different paces or times of the day, season and *dosha*. Thus, music therapy can be tailored to one's *dosha*, time of day, and season.

Most Indian grocery stores throughout the US sell meditational music for the time of day and season, as well as the general *ragas* for all times and people. Music from the more popular artists like Ravi Shankar and Ali Akbar Khan can be found in most large record stores.

Aromatherapy

Therapeutic aromas are used in several forms—incense, essential oils, soap, sachets and scented candles. As one inhales a pleasant aroma, the response is, 'mmm, that smells good'. Instantly the mind has a pleasurable experience. One value of this experience is that the frame of mind is changed to a more pleasant outlook. Aromas can be classified according to *dosha*. For example, sandalwood is good for all *doshas*, making the mind calm and alert.

Aromas are also used for specific health concerns. For example, Jasmine, patchouli and ylang-ylang are specifically used to help break depression. Frankincense kills germs in the air (e.g., cold and flu germs). Lavender calms hyperactive children. Many restaurants are aware of the effects of aromas and are now using aromatherapy to enhance the ambiance of their establishments.

Below are aroma lists for each *dosha*.

Vata

sandalwood	rose	jasmine
cedar	lily	vanilla
lavender	sage	patchouli
basil	myrrh	frankincense
musk	lotus	eucalyptus
cinnamon		

Pitta

sandalwood	rose	jasmine
lily	vanilla	lavender
geranium	gardenia	lemongrass

Kapha

sandalwood	patchouli	Basil
myrrh	sage	cedar
frankincense	musk	Lotus
eucalyptus	cinnamon	

Color Therapy

Colors play an important role in creating a pleasant mood. Hospitals and restaurants are aware of how colors affect the emotions of clients. Color therapy can be used in clothes, home, and office furnishings (eg, paint, carpets, paintings, and flowers. Ayurveda offers color categorization for each *dosha*. Healing colors are bright and pleasant, not dull or murky. Below is a list of colors best suited for each *dosha*.

Vata

white	sky blue	turquoise
gold	yellow	pink
some red		

These colors calm anxiety, worry, fear, and nervousness.

Pitta

white	sky blue	turquoise
pink	emerald green	

Kapha

red	orange	yellow
gold		

Summary

Meditation, music, aroma, and color therapies specifically calm and balance the mental, emotional, and spiritual imbalances such as stress, worry, anger, and lethargy. Since many physical diseases are psychosomatic, it is important to enjoy these therapies on a daily basis.

Chapter 8

Pancha Karma:
Five Unique Ayurvedic Healing Therapies

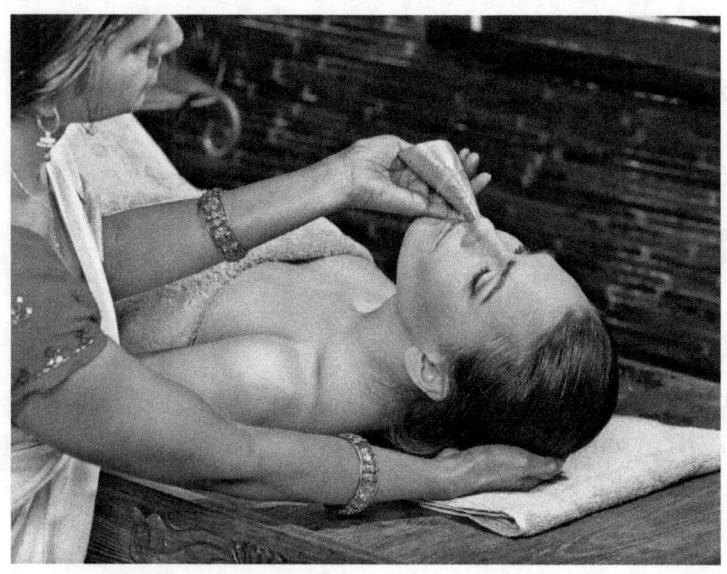

We have discussed the unique cleansing, healing, prevention, and longevity therapies offered through Ayurveda. Yet some extremely severe diseases require stronger therapies if they are to be healed. For this, Ayurveda offers *Pancha karma* (five actions).

The value of *pancha karma* is that it completely removes toxins from the body. In this way, a complete healing can occur. *Pancha karma* is often recommended for healing and prevention, but perhaps its most dramatic results come from healing diseases believed to be incurable. You can stand outside of various *pancha karma* clinics in India, watching people being carried or wheeled into the clinic, too weak to stand on their own. After several weeks of treatment these people walk out of the clinic on their own two feet.

These five healing therapies comprise a simple yet extensive process. Below we will just discuss the basic theory behind *pancha karma*.

Section One of this book discussed the origin sites of the three *doshas*. The stomach is where all Kapha disorders develop before spreading to other parts of the body. The origin site for Pitta is the small intestine. Vata's home site is the colon. *Pancha karma* provides a three-step process to return the toxins to the home site. Like playing a movie in reverse, toxins move backward to their origin site before being completely expelled from the body.

The first stage of *pancha karma* is the preparatory level. This consists of a moderated diet, body oil massage and steam treatments. The diet is both toning and detoxifying. The oil massage and steam begin to dislodge and liquefy toxins, returning them to the blood stream. Some of the toxins are expelled through the pores of the skin during the steam therapy. The remaining toxins flow through the blood stream back to their site of origin.

Once the toxins have returned home, persons are ready for the second stage of *pancha karma*. This is the actual *pancha karma* processes. Generally, a person only requires one of the five *pancha karma* treatments. Discussed below are each of the five therapies.

Kapha excesses return to the stomach. Once there, they are expelled from the body through a special herbally-induced emetic procedure called *vamana*. The easiest and closest route out of the body from the stomach is the mouth. Special steps are taken to induce vomiting the toxins from the body.

Pitta excesses return to the small intestine. Simple purgatives flush these toxins out of the body via bowel movements. This process is called *virechana*. Vata excesses return to the colon. Flushing Vata toxins from this organ requires various forms of herbal and oil enemas called *basti*.

Once the toxins are completely removed from these three origin sites, a brief period of rest and rejuvenation is required to begin to build healthy cells and tissues in the body, while adjusting to this healthy state of balance. Proper diet, rest, meditation, and other useful therapies are followed for a set time. This is the final stage, post-*pancha karma*.

The remaining two *pancha karma* therapies are application of herb powders and oils through the nose (*nasya*) and blood-letting (*rakta moksha*). Nasya is highly effective for healing disorders of the head and mind. *Rakta moksha* is used in cases of highly toxic blood (this system is not often used outside of India.).

This five-step process dislodges and removes the deepest-seated toxins that may not be removed from other therapies. Thus, even diseases thought to be incurable can be removed from the body.

Summary

Pancha karma is a unique process that complete removes the deepest-seated toxins from the body—useful in chronic conditions thought to be incurable.

Chapter 9 External Influences:
Climate/season, Buildings, Astrology

In order to be truly holistic in nature, Ayurveda discusses both internal and external causes of imbalance. In the past chapters, we have reviewed internal causes and therapeutic suggestions. This chapter will discuss conditions that can cause imbalance from outside the body.

Climate and season are discussed in the Ayurvedic texts. Indian or Vedic astrology (*Jyotish*) was once a part of Ayurveda but later became its own separate science. *Jyotish* discusses how the planets affect mental and physical health, career, relationships, and spiritual life. Building houses, offices, and temples, according to the laws of nature is another Vedic science called *Vastu Shastra*. These sciences are briefly discussed below to illustrate how they affect one's health and well-being.

Climate and Season

The Ayurvedic definition of health stated in Chapter 1 is a state of dynamic balance. This means that as life factors change, balance must be monitored. Following one's Ayurvedic diet and lifestyle is not always enough to remain balanced. Weather conditions can tip the equilibrium if ignored.

Like foods, herbs, aromas, etc. seasons are related to the *doshas*. The cold, dry windy weather of fall and winter are more Vata seasons (Kapha may also be bothered by the cold). In the spring, when the weather warms and the snow and ice melt so do toxins in the body. The excess fluids aggravates Kapha *dosha*. The heat of the summer brings with it an excess of Pitta. In some places the dry heat of summer also adds to the dryness of Vata.

As the seasons change, their effect on the body and mind can become apparent. Persons need to adjust their habits accordingly to remain balanced. For example, all *doshas* may be able to digest raw vegetables in the summer.

However, in the winter, even Pitta *doshas* may requires steamed vegetables. In the winter when colds and flus abound Kapha *dosha* is excessed. All *doshas* may need to have some hotter spices to keep Kapha in balance.

Climates vary from region to region and country to country. Those who live near the equator or tropical climates have more Pitta climates to contend with. The rainy seasons in many countries can aggravate all three *doshas*. Those living in humid, muggy climates must also consider these factors when balancing their lives. Mountain regions must contend with wind, cold, and sun. Thus, climate and season require consideration for holistic health to prevail.

Jyotish - Vedic Astrology

We are aware of how certain planets affect the earth and her people. The full Moon causes high tides and strong emotions. The sun causes heat, Sun burns and skin cancer. According to *Jyotish* each planet also affects people more subtly, depending upon each planet's vibratory rate.

When a planet is strong and beneficial, as reflected in a person's birth chart clear, positive situations will be noticed. If a planet is strongly unfavorable, problems will be reflected in one's life. *Jyotish* looks at the four main areas of life, health, life purpose (*dharma*) and wealth; relationships, and spiritual life. Below are a list of the main planets considered in *Jyotish* and their beneficial and harmful effects.

Sun: <u>Favorable</u>- qualities of independence, strong sense of self. <u>Unfavorable</u>- low self-worth, drive or motivation; low energy, anemia, poor digestion, heart, or circulation.

Moon: <u>Favorable</u>- Nurturing, healing, balanced emotions.
<u>Unfavorable</u>- emotional instability, depression, moody; anemia, weak lungs

and kidneys, menstrual difficulties.

Mars: Favorable- Strong leadership qualities, courage, energetic, strong. Unfavorable- Lack of energy, passive, controlled, abused; weak immune system, strength, and liver.

Mercury: Favorable- Creative, healing, writing, communication abilities. Unfavorable- Weak skills in the above areas, education difficulties; weak nervous system, digestion, lungs, and heart; nervous and anxious. Possible financial difficulties.

Jupiter: Favorable- Enthusiastic, spiritual, expansive, graceful. Unfavorable- Lack of the above qualities, depression, infertile, poor immune system, liver, pancreas, absorption, nerves and glands. Possible financial difficulties.

Venus: Favorable- Charm, beauty, grace,

artistic.

Unfavorable- Lack of the above qualities, weak kidneys, reproductive system, immune system. Possible financial difficulties.

Saturn: Favorable- Calm, grounded, balanced.
Unfavorable- Fear, anxiety, weak bones, nerves, vitality, longevity, mysterious diseases (e.g., cancer, epilepsy, paralysis).

Rahu (Moon's north node)
Favorable- Clarity, influential, spiritual insights.
Unfavorable- Illusions, fear, anxiety, out of touch with

self and others; weak immune system, mysterious diseases (e.g., cancer, epilepsy, paralysis).

Ketu (Moon's south node):

<u>Favorable</u>- Clarity, sense of freedom, spiritual insights.
<u>Unfavorable</u>- Poor perception, self-destructive, accidents, feeling constricted; poor digestion, circulation, ulcers, nerves, mysterious diseases (e.g., cancer, epilepsy, and paralysis).

The 12 houses of the birth chart relate to the different areas of life. Integrating the strength and meaning of planets with the house meanings results in clearer understandings of the areas of one's life and health. Below are the 12 houses and some of their meanings.

1. Personality, health 2. Education, livelihood potential 3. Socializing, courage 4. Home, mother, property, possessions 5. Creativity, children 6. Physical health 7. Relationship/ Marriage 8. Mental health 9. Life purpose

(*dharma*), spiritual purpose
10. Career   11. Wealth, spiritual gains
12. Losses, spiritual liberation

A birth chart is constructed based upon one's birth time, place, and date. Everyone has some strong and weak planets. Therapies are offered to offset the planetary weaknesses. These include mantras, herbs, talismans, and lifestyle suggestions.

Astrology is not for everybody. Due to the superficial level presented in society skepticism is understandable.

Integrating *Jyotish* with Ayurveda is useful when dealing with very serious diseases or when a person has many unrelated health problems occurring simultaneously. The value of *Jyotish* in relation to Ayurveda is in offering a wider set of possibilities that cause health disorders.

Buildings

Ayurveda is in effect the laws of nature in the area of health. *Jyotish* astrology offers the laws of nature corresponding to the planets. *Vedic* architecture (*Vastu Shastra*) represents the laws of nature as they relate to architecture. This science completes the triad of the three sciences. It harmonizes the human, the cosmos, and the earth.

Vastu Shastra considers the earth's magnetic

fields, the solar rays, the color spectrum, and more, and how a living structure reflects these environmental influences on humans. Some examples of *Vastu Shastra* rules include having the driveway, front door, and bedroom windows face the east.

This way the healing and warming sun rays best influence humans. Of course, this science discusses subtler benefits as well. Thousands of years ago when this science was committed to writing, they discussed the seven rays of the sun which correspond to the spectrum of the rainbow. Modern science has found the same information with technology while the ancient *Vedic* architects learned this information through their meditations.

Other rays and influences discussed by *Vastu Shastra* have yet to be discovered by modern science.

Vastu Shastra says that inhabitants of a home, office, or store built according to the rules of Vastu will remain healthy and prosperous. The texts also discuss methods to lay out an entire town or city according to natural law. Many people today are becoming more interested in environmentally safe building.

Vastu Shastra brings this idea to completion. One popular version of *Vastu Shastra* is the Chinese architectural system of *Feng Shui* (pronounced *fung shway*). Through the use of inexpensive building therapies like mirrors, crystals, and wind chimes persons can easily offset structural conditions that can cause health, career or relationship problems.

Summary

This chapter reviewed environmental considerations that can influence one's mental and physical health, career, relationship, and spiritual life. By considering both internal and external causes of imbalance persons have a handle on the whole range of life influences. Control over one's health is easily possible with this complete perspective.

Section III: Case Studies & Scientific Research

Chapter 10 Case Studies

Below are some reports from various clients who tell us about the results of following their Ayurvedic recommend- ations. These stories help illustrate how Ayurvedic consultations and therapies are applied and how clients experience beneficial results quickly, without side effects, and inexpensively.

The cost for all therapies described below range from $2 to $25 per month. Readers may compare these prices with the monthly cost of each corresponding allopathic treatment.

Winter colds & flu:

One of the biggest winter problems in our area of the country aside from shoveling snow is dealing with the spreading of colds and various strains of the flu. Especially troubling to our clients is having their children catch the flu at school and infect the other family members. Just as one child recovers, their sister or brother come down with the same symptoms.

This is generally a Kapha excess condition. We recommend a formula including ginger and *pippali*, two warming herbs to dry up the excess fluids, and *vasak* and *bala* to strengthen the lungs. Some of the herbs also boost the immune system. By keeping excess Kapha out of the system during the winter, parents report their children do not contract the flu. At the first sign of sniffles even parents take these herbs to prevent illness.

We have several people making delivery of mail and packages to our center. Inevitably they make a delivery on a winter day walking around with a cold or sore throat. Jumping in and out of the truck, walking in cold, rainy, snowy weather takes a toll on their health and immune system. All of our regular delivery people are now regular users of this cold and flu formula.

One delivery person came in with a very bad sore throat. He was given the herbs and told to drink them in a cup of tea. The next time he brought us a delivery he related in amazement how his sore throat went away as he was drinking the tea.

Arthritis:

A client of ours called and asked about their mother who was in her 80's. Most of her adult life she had severe, painful arthritis. Since she had a Vata *dosha* and Vata arthritis symptoms we gave her *yogaraj guggul* to take internally. She also massaged the *mahanarayan* herbal oil into her skin wherever there was pain. Her son also encouraged her to stop eating meat as this was also aggravating the condition.

She reported that as soon as she put the oil on her hands the pain went away for several hours at a time. This woman was amazed to find herself living without pain for the first time in decades. Around a year later I called to see how she was doing. No longer taking the herbs or oil, the woman reported that she was 99% healthy; she had no arthritic problems.

Diabetes:

A call came into the center one day from a man with diabetes. He was using the internet news group for alternative diabetic discussion. A person mentioned the Ayurvedic herb *gurmar* had helped him with his diabetes. The caller began to look for someone who had this herb. Finally, he was referred to our center. We suggested *gurmar* for removing sugar from the pancreas and *shilajit* to heal the kidney. He ordered the herbs and began taking them. Shortly thereafter he called to tell us how well he felt and that he was posting our center's name and his experiences with the alternative diabetes news group. We get calls from readers of this group from around the country.

Acne:

One of our clients is a holistic cosmetic aesthetician. She came to see us because she had severe acne herself. We suggested several herbs to cleanse the skin and blood (*manjishtha* and turmeric). She then received a nutritional consultation. It is not enough to merely focus on clearing the skin; the body's toxins that cause the acne need to be removed as well.

She came back only a week later smiling to show us how well her skin was clearing up. At the same time, she mentioned that she was feeling healthier and stronger from eating properly.

Breast cancer:

A woman in her late 30's wanted An Ayurvedic consultation for cancer. We gave her a number of herbs to cleanse the blood, improve blood circulation and boost her immune system. Herbs included *manjishtha, bala,* and *guggul.* We spoke of the idea that cancer is related to a loss of purpose in life. She immediately confirmed this is how she felt. Her profession was acting in plays. We spoke about what she loves to do and she felt compelled to try directing plays. More than two years later she reports having a cancer-free, great life.

About six months later the doctors ran the usual tests and found no trace of the cancer. Also, she began directing. She still needed the herbs but said her health and life were completely transformed.

Prostate Cancer: One of the graduates of our Ayurveda certification program called about one of their clients. His prostate cancer confined him to bed; he wasn't strong enough to work. His prostate doctor told him there was nothing more that could be done for him medically so he decided to try an Ayurvedic approach. Many of the same herbs mentioned above were given to this man. He was also given a food plan according to his *dosha* and *dharmic* and spiritual counseling was also offered.

Within a week, he began to feel so healthy and energetic he let himself become over active. Returning to his old habits and foods, his energy relapsed. Now he took the Ayurvedic suggestions seriously and quickly returned to health. He even began working again. When his prostate doctor saw these results, he called the practitioner who graduated from our course to ask about the treatment. As the phone call ended he referred another of his patients for an Ayurvedic consultation. This second man had such good results that he became involved with the practitioner's center and helped develop the practice.

Anemia:

We've had numerous female clients for anemia. Nutritional suggestions included eating iron-rich foods like black grapes, cane sugar, and sesame seeds. Herbs included *chyavan prash*, saffron, *manjishtha, shatavari,* and *punarnava* .

These clients were especially happy because they received frequent blood tests from their doctors who could scientifically validate the rebuilding of healthy red blood cells. Within a year all these clients had recovered from anemia.

One of these clients had a secondary problem, excess menstruation that caused further depletion of the much-needed blood.

This was a Pitta-excess disorder. She was given a Pitta reduction food plan and astringent herbs like red raspberry. Astringent tastes are constrictive and stop bleeding. This case required a twofold approach to healing the anemia.

Parasites:

We have had numerous clients developing parasites. Many contracted them from visiting India and Africa. One 67 family moved here from Israel and developed parasites from American foods. Parasites thrive in moist, damp climate. Anti-parasitical food plans require the avoidance of any foods that increase Kapha. Yeast-free breads, avoidance of dairy (except *lassi* and *ghee*) and sugars are required. Purgatives begin to flush the parasites out of the system. Vata and Kapha *doshas* take hot spices like cloves to kill parasites through heat. All *doshas* take anti-parasitical herbs like *kutaj* which directly destroy the parasites. Immune boosting herbs like *guduchi* and *shilajit* are also needed. Parasitical conditions require a twofold approach of anti-parasitical herbs and foods, and immune boosting herbs.

Persons with this condition have to more carefully follow their food plan. It seems that even the slightest increase of moist foods help build the parasite population. Clients reported an easing of their symptoms within a few days of beginning their Ayurvedic recommendations.

Allergies:

Seasonal allergies affect a wide portion of the population. We have found that the main cause of allergies is a weak digestive system, and improper diet and weak immune system. Ayurvedic therapies for this condition are somewhat amusing to recommend because no specific anti- allergy herbs are given. Clients ask in wonder, 'aren't you going to give me any herbs for my allergies?'. The answer is always, 'no, just by following these food recommendations for your *dosha* and taking digestive spices (like cardamom or coriander) and immune-boosting herbs, you will find your allergies reducing'. Many of these clients report their allergies are almost completely gone after only one week of following the suggestions.

Cholesterol:

Another case verified by modern science came to us from the owner of a clothing business. His doctor told him his cholesterol levels were too high. We gave him *yogaraj guggul* and advised him to have little or no animal products. Every few months he would call to tell us the results of his cholesterol tests; levels consistently reduced until his cholesterol returned to normal.

Weightloss:

Perhaps one of the greatest concerns among people, weightloss is actually one of the trickiest disorders to balance. We created a formula using some of the main weightloss herbs including *garcinia, triphala, tulsi*, ginger, and *Katakura*. Results seem to be common with all clients. First noticed is a reduction of water in the system. People look thinner even before the weight is reduced. The next three to four months most clients report gradual but consistent weight reduction.

After about four months the metabolism

tricks the body and does not allow further weight reduction for some time. Clients report that even though they are at a plateau for several months they do not gain weight. After a three to four month plateau the weight begins to drop again.

Weightloss is more easily achieved when clients follow their Ayurvedic *dosha* diet and follow some sort of exercise program—even if it is only walking for 1/2 hour three times weekly.

Uterine Fibroids/Ovarian Cysts:

While many clients have come to us with this condition, it seems the majority are women who moved to the US recently, live in the city, and are experiencing the stresses of city life along with an unfamiliar (and unhealthy diet).

The formula we use includes the herbs *shatavari, ashok, dahlia, musta, manjishtha, kakamachi, amalaki* and *haridra*. Other suggestions include proper diet and taking walks by the water or in forests or parks to attune oneself with nature. The symptoms begin to disappear within a week or two. Reports from their doctors find the disappearance of the fibroids. Sonograms show ovarian cysts shrinking and disappearing within 2 to 5 months [5/21/97; 7/16/97; 10/12/97].

PMS:

This is the most common problem with women during menstrual cycle years. Anger and impatience are symptoms of Pitta-excessed PMS. Cold limbs, dizziness, cramps, and anxiety are symptoms of Vata excessive PMS. These are the two most common sets of symptoms we hear. The same herbs used for uterine fibroids above are used for PMS. Clients report relief within 1 week. Each person is also advised to follow his or her Ayurvedic dosha food plan.

Menopause:

This is another common disorder of our clients. The same herbal formula and food suggestions used above are given for these symptoms. One woman was so pleased with the results that she organized a lecture at our local library to introduce the Ayurvedic concept to the community.

Morning Sickness:

We have found red raspberry leaves to be a quick and effective therapy for all forms of nausea including morning sickness. The best experience we had was with a woman whose chiropractor referred her to us. He tried many therapies to relieve her nausea but to no avail.

This woman was carrying her second child. Her symptoms were the same as when she was pregnant with her first baby. She became so nauseous that she couldn't eat anything at any time of the day or night. Even a taste of food from a spoon would produce emesis. She was frightened, not wanting to undergo the same situation as during her first pregnancy.

When she came for a consultation she was given 1/4 teaspoon of red raspberry leaf powder and some water to wash it down. After about a minute she was asked how she felt. Her response was, 'If I am not sick now, it won't make me sick; I can eat this herb'.

Herbal tonics to strengthen her immune system and her baby's immunity were suggested. By this time, she was so excited that she could eat something and not get sick that she became child-like. She jumped up and followed the practitioner to sample the tonic (*chyavan prash*), eagerly smiling. This was quite a change from the frightened looking woman who first entered the center.

The tonic was also successfully eaten. Happy and hopeful, she took these products home with her. A few weeks later a mutual friend of hers and ours was at the center. I asked how the woman was doing. She was living a healthy life; her eating habits were back to normal.

Childbirth:

Several of our pregnant clients took herbs to boost their immune systems in order to have more energy during pregnancy. Along with the *chyavan prash* tonic, they took herbs including *shatavari*. Not only did they report a great boost in energy from the herbs, but also when the baby was born, they were extremely healthy with lustrous eyes. [Do not take herbs during pregnancy without the guidance of a knowledgeable health care practitioner]

Mental:

Whether discussing anxiety, fear, worry, anger, impatience, or lethargy, mental stress is the most common concern among our clients. Our herbal therapy includes gotu kola, *ashwagandha, bhringaraj, shank pushpi, bala* and sandalwood. Clients report that results are almost immediate.

We also discuss home, career and life habits that seem to create the stress and suggest more constructive habits and thought patterns.

Ayurvedic Pet Therapy

Yes, pets also react well to Ayurvedic herbs. In fact, they are extremely sensitive. Intuitively they know the herbs are helpful. Many clients report that when they bring home the bag or bottle of herbs their cat or dog attack the contents trying to eat them. Below are some illustrations of how Ayurveda is applied when healing animals.

Dogs

Kidney tumor- One Scotty was diagnosed with a large malignant tumor on their liver. It seems to be a disease common to Scotties. The veterinarian could do nothing and gave the dog about one month to live. The Scotty's owners brought the dog to our center. The main herbs given were *manjishtha* and *guggul*. Other herbs were given for secondary symptoms such as liver infection, cough etc. Spiritual counseling was offered to the clients, discussing the true nature of humans and animals are their eternal soul. Counseling was provided to help the dog's owners to better deal with the life and death issues with their pet.

The Scotty loved the herbs. Within a few days, the dog was becoming healthier and livelier. The dog lived in good general health for an entire year. During one of his medical checkups the veterinarian was amazed to find the liver infection had completely healed. One day the dog simply stopped eating the herbs and peacefully died a few days later. The owners were better able to accept their Scotty's passing and were glad he was able to live in general good health for much longer than the veterinarian had predicted.

Skin parasites/skin patches- The Scotty's owners referred another family with a Scotty to our center. The dog was constantly biting and scratching his skin. Hair was falling out in clumps. The vet diagnosed the dog with some sort of skin parasites. We gave the dog *manjishtha* for blood and skin purification and *kutaj*, the best anti- parasitical herb. Within a few weeks, the condition was completely healed. We have had similar success with many dogs and cats with this condition.

Bladder Sand/Incontinence- Several dogs

were diagnosed with bladder sand by their vets. We gave them *gokshura* and within a day or two the incontinence cleared up. By their next check-up at the vet the sand was gone.

Cats

Bronchitis- We have had several cats with bronchitis. The same herbs given to people for colds and flu (above) are successfully used for this condition.

Emotional Imbalance- One cat owner had an emotional breakup of a relationship. The cat seemed to reflect the trauma of the experience. Gotu kola was given to the cat to calm his mind. Rose flowers were given to calm the emotions and heart. When the owner brought the bag of herbs home the cat jumped on the table, tore through the bag and began eating the herbs. His emotions began to become balanced in a few days.

Horses

Infection/Inflammation- The owners of the Scotty referred our center to their sister who breeds horses. Their two most common health concerns were inflammation and infection, and colds. We gave the horses herbal antibiotics like turmeric and *guduchi* for the infections. Herbs for the colds included *pippali*, ginger, and *vasak*. The horses are responding very well to the herbs and the breeder now orders the herbs in large quantities.

Summary

These case studies briefly show how Ayurveda theory and therapies are applied.

Further, the cases reveal just how effective Ayurvedic therapies can be, and that none of the clients experienced side effects. Patients, doctors, and insurance companies would be well advised to investigate this well-tested health care system, which has the additional benefit of cost effectiveness.

Chapter 11 Scientific Research

We have discussed the uniqueness of Ayurvedic theory, diagnosis, and therapies. The simple, effective and personalized method of finding the root cause of an illness and the healing of disorders has been detailed. The Ayurvedic process of healing diseases currently believed to be incurable (like epilepsy, asthma and arthritis) has also been explained.

In the last chapter case studies were cited to

illustrate the application of Ayurveda and how results are experienced. This ancient science is meeting with great interest and enthusiasm. Yet being a society seeking proof of claims, it will be useful to examine some scientific research on various Ayurvedic herbs. Pubmed (https://www.ncbi.nlm.nih.gov/pubmed/) is the NIH (National Institutes of Health) international database of research abstracts. Thousands of abstracts on Ayurvedic herb studies are available. Many of the studies involved animal testing while others used proprietary products. Below is discussed the first research project in the US that measured cost savings between Ayurveda and allopathy. Thereafter research on specific herbs is examined.

Saving Insurance Companies Money

In a preliminary study on seasonal allergies, 5 subjects received Ayurvedic consultations and received a combination of herbs, spices and nutritional therapies. In all cases allergy relief began within two days to two weeks. This holistic approach found non-allergy health disorders also clearing up.

Longitudinal and prevention measurements were available for two of the subjects for 4- & 5-year periods. It was found that as long as the subjects followed their Ayurvedic nutritional suggestions and took the appropriate spices, no seasonal allergy symptoms ever occurred. Only when they stopped their therapies did they begin to develop allergy symptoms.

Cost comparisons found that over a 6-month allergy season, Ayurveda subjects spent between $0 to $147, while average costs for allergists, OTC or prescribed allergy medication cost $535 for the same 6-month allergy season (if no side effects were experienced) and $735 to $1,070 (with side effects).

With health care cost reductions being realized through Ayurvedic therapies, insurance costs can be significantly reduced. This should please both the insurance companies and their customers.

Herb Research

There are thousands of scientific studies on Ayurvedic herbs. Below is a partial list of herbs and the areas of health they have been found to benefit as indicated by the various scientific studies. However, before we proceed it is important to discuss current research methodology. These herbs have been used effectively in India for more than 5,000 years. Their safety is thus documented from an extensive life-experience point of view. Therefore, herb studies on humans should not pose any fears. However, the majority of studies are performed on animals. It is the view of this author that animal studies are at once unnecessary and cruel, and are not encouraged.

The second point is that a larger number of studies are being conducted on isolated active ingredients of the herbs. This has resulted in herb companies in the US selling herbal products with only the isolated active ingredient in extract form. There are two potentially dangerous outcomes from ingesting isolated active ingredients, and also from ingesting extracts.

We need to remember that allopathic drugs are basically nothing more than the isolated active ingredients of herbs (when using nonsynthetic forms). It is also crucial to bear in mind that prescription drugs have become the fourth leading cause of death in the US today (2-1/2 times as many deaths as from AIDS and roughly the equivalent of one 747 plane crash a day).

The point is that Mother Nature has made an herb with not only the active ingredient, but with various other ingredients that are natural protectors against side effects. Once humans start tampering with nature, the herbal products can become as harmful and as deadly as allopathic drugs. In short, it behooves the holistic community, including herb and pharmaceutical companies to not let herbal research and sale of product become a slave of the allopathic mindset of what is healthy. Once the herbs are treated in the same light as allopathic drugs, the life-force and holistic integrity of herbs will be destroyed and the end products can become harmful.

The common western mindset that is misguided is the notion that if something is good for you, then the more you take, the quicker you'll get better. Again, Ayurveda has found that just a little of an herb is enough to stimulate the body and mind to initiate the healing process.

From the spiritual point of view, health is a spiritual condition. Material objects like a bit of an herb can help inspire the material blocks to be removed, but healing is achieved through inspiring the spirit or soul.

Therefore, use of large amounts of herbs, or using concentrated forms of herbs in extract form, keep the focus of healing, incorrectly on the herb as a material object. Further, by using isolated active herbal ingredients that have a potentially harmful effect, and then concentrating this effect into extract form, there may now a recipe for greater danger in the use of these products.

In our own center, we've had numerous clients tell us of the side effects they had from taking extracts and isolated active ingredient herbal products. Hopefully the concern for health will outweigh the need for allopathic approval or economic profits.

Some make a case for standardized herbal products in the name of accurate measurement; they make the assumption that standardized herbs automatically means 'quality and dependability'. However, after standardization, in addition the harmful effects mentioned above, companies can add the lowest quality of ingredients as the remainder of the product, thereby offering an overall inferior and possibly harmful formula.

Therefore, it is the suggestion of Ayurveda to use whole plants, and where needed, whole-plant extracts in the healing process. Let us heed the warning to keep the integrity of Ayurvedic medicine as a healing life-force, and not sell out to allopathic health paradigms in the name of high sales profits. Nearly half the population has moved to alternative healing, this tells us that allopathic medicine, while having many benefits, does not have all the answers.

Lastly it can be remembered that herbal medicine use costs between $2 and $20 per month supply (when used 1/4 tsp. 3 times daily for individual herbs). Mild doses of whole herbs are safe, inexpensive and highly effective.

Below is a list of scientific research on herbs, and the area of healing they benefit. Some studies were done using whole plants, some on whole plant extracts, some on isolated active ingredient. Some studies were on humans and others on animals or in-vitro. All studies listed here are merely to show the overwhelming evidence of the effectiveness of Ayurvedic herbs; this in no way should be construed to suggest the advocacy of animal studies or isolated ingredients as a method of research or approach to taking herbal products.

aloe vera- wound healing-34/ anti-inflammatory-34a

amalaki-acute pancreatitis-10

amalaki/haritaki/bibhitaki-cholesterol-induced atherosclerosis-10a

amalaki/bibhitaki/haritaki/amlavedasa (yellow dock)-HIV-24/ antimicrobial-24a

arjuna-antianginal, cardioprotective-13 & 13a/ angina pectoris 13C/cardiac tonic and current uses include treatment for angina, hypertension, arrhythmia's, and congestive heart failure. 21

arjuna/guggul-ischemic heart disease

(inadequate blood flow to heart leading to angina pectoris/heart attack)-13d cancer-13b/

arjuna, nirgundi-anti-bacterial-9

ashwagandha/shilajit-cognition enhancing memory Alzheimer's-2a/antioxidant-2b

bakuchi-nutritional source of genistein and daidzein isoflavones-18/asthma-18a

bhumyamalaki-HIV 30 & 30a bilwa-antifungal-16

black pepper-anti-bacterial/penicillin-15/antioxidant-15a

black pepper/cumin-colon cancer-36

brihati-antitumor-38

chirayata-antimicrobial-1/hypoglycemia-1a/12b

cinnamon/cumin-anti-bacterial-11

coriander-cholesterol/triglicerides-11a

cumin/basal-anti-carcinogenic-12

cumin/turmeric-anti-atherosclerosis, anti-inflammatory, antithrombotic-40

fenugreek-diabetes-32

ginger-nausea, vomiting, headache, arteriosclerosis-41, 41b/rheumatism-41a

ginger./pippali/coriander/musta/cumin/cinnamon/asafetida/triphala-indigestion-41c

gotu kola - psoriasis - 22/ antioxidant/memory enhancing, epilepsy, insomnia, sedative-22a

gotu kola/shankpushpi/ashwagandha/licorice/vacha/sarpagandha-schizophrenia-22b guduchi-immunity-26/ liver disease 26a/jaundice 26b/diabetes type II -29/ joint swelling in adjuvant arthritis-37

guduchi/turmeric/bilwa/karella-urinary tract infections- 26c

guggul-cholesterol/atherosclerosis-19, 19a/superior to nitroglycerin-reducing chest pain and dyspnea of angina-21

gurmar-suppression of sweet tastes-12a, 12b/diabetes-27

gurmar/neem/shilajit-diabetes-27a

haritaki/bhringaraj/tulsi-antibacterial-23

ishabgol-irritable bowel syndrome-17

kapikachu-Parkinson's-8/ diabetes-33

kushta-anti-tumor-7/hepatitis B-7a/kutki-hepatitis B-31

licorice- antimicrobial-42/atherosclerosis-42a/anti-viral-encephalitis-42b

manjishtha-anti-tumor-6-6a/ antioxidant-6b/ antiviral-6c

neem-malaria, anti-parasitical-4 nirgundi-anti-inflammatory-5a

punarnava/guduchi/haritaki/ginger/barberry -immunity/T- cells-25/liver-25a

punarnava/bhringaraj/chirayata/arogyavardhini/mandur bhasma-liver/bile-25b

saffron-antitumor-35

shatavari-gastric emptying time-3

shilajit-peptic ulcers and anti-inflammatory-2, 28

trikatu -absorption/bioavailability-14

turmeric-gallstones, cholesterol-

20/ibuprofen substitute,
    anti-inflammatory-20a/anti-carcinogenic-20
    B/anti-inflammatory, antispasmodic, liver/bile-39
turmeric and cumin-cancer lesions-20c/antitumor-20d

References

1-Omoregbe RE, Ikuebe OM, Ihimire IG. Anti-microbial activity of some medicinal plants extracts on Escherichia coli, Salmonella paratyphi and Shigella dysenteriae. Afr J Med Med Sci 1996 Dec;25(4):373-5

1a-Karunanayake EH, Welihinda J, Sirimanne SR, Sinnadorai G. Oral hypoglycaemic activity of some medicinal plants of Sri Lanka. J Ethnopharmacol 1984 Jul;11(2):223-31

2-Goel RK, Banerjee RS, Acharya SB. Antiulcerogenic and anti-inflammatory studies with shilajit. J Ethnopharmacol 1990 Apr;29(1):95-103 2a-Schliebs R, Liebmann A, Bhattacharya SK, Kumar A, Ghosal S, Bigl V. (Indian Ginseng) and Shilajit differentially affects cholinergic but not glutamatergic and GABAergic markers in rat brain. Systemic administration of defined extracts from Withania somnifera. Neurochem Int 1997 Feb;30(2):181-90 2b-Bhattacharya SK, Satyan KS, Ghosal S. Antioxidant activity of glycowithanolides from Withania somnifera. Indian J Exp Biol 1997 Mar;35(3):236-9

3-Dalvi SS, Nadkarni PM, Gupta KC. Effect of Asparagus racemosus (Shatavari) on gastric emptying time in normal healthy volunteers. J Postgrad Med 1990 Apr;36(2):91-4 4-Dhar R, Zhang K, Talwar GP, Garg S, Kumar N. Inhibition of the growth and development of asexual and sexual stages of drug-sensitive and resistant strains of the human malaria parasite Plasmodium falciparum by Neem (Azadirachta indica) fractions. J Ethnopharmacol 1998 May;61(1):31-9

5-Chawla AS, Sharma AK, Handa SS, Dhar KL. Chemical investigation and anti-inflammatory activity of Vitex negundo seeds. J Nat Prod 1992 Feb;55(2):163-7 6-Takeya K, Yamamiya T, Morita H, Itokawa H. Two antitumour bicyclic hexapeptides from Rubia cordifolia. Phytochemistry 1993 Jun;33(3):613-5

6a-Adwankar MK, Chitnis MP. In vivo anti-cancer activity of RC-18: a plant isolate from Rubia cordifolia, Linn. against a spectrum of experimental tumor models. Chemotherapy 1982;28(4):291-3

6b-Tripathi YB, Sharma M, Manickam M.

Rubiadin, a new antioxidant from Rubia cordifolia. Indian J Biochem Biophys 1997 Jun;34(3):302-6 6c-Ho LK, Don MJ, Chen HC, Yeh SF, Chen JM. Inhibition of hepatitis B surface antigen secretion on human hepatoma cells. Components from Rubia cordifolia. J Nat Prod 1996 Mar;59(3):330-3

7-Cho JY, Park J, Yoo ES, Baik KU, Jung JH, Lee J, Park MH. Inhibitory effect of sesquiterpene lactones from Saussurea lappa on tumor necrosis factor-alpha production in murine macrophage-like cells. Planta Med 1998 Oct;64(7):594-7

7a-Chen HC, Chou CK, Lee SD, Wang JC, Yeh SF. Active compounds from Saussurea lappa Clarks that suppress 81

hepatitis B virus surface antigen gene expression in human hepatoma cells. Antiviral Res 1995 May;27(1-2):99-

109 8-An alternative medicine treatment for Parkinson's disease: results of a multi-center clinical trial. HP-200 in Parkinson's Disease Study Group. J Altern Complement Med 1995 Fall;1(3):249-55

9-Perumal Samy R, Ignacimuthu S, Sen A. Screening of 34 Indian medicinal plants for antibacterial properties. J Ethnopharmacol 1998 Sep;62(2):173-82 10-Thorat SP, Rege NN, Naik AS, Thatte UM, Joshi A, Panicker KN, Bapat RD, Dahanukar SA

Emblica officinalis: a novel therapy for acute pancreatitis-- an experimental study. HPB Surg 1995;9(1):25-30 10a-Thakur CP, Thakur B, Singh S, Sinha PK, Sinha SK. The Ayurvedic medicines Haritaki, Amala and Bahira reduce cholesterol-induced atherosclerosis in rabbits. Int J Cardiol 1988 Nov;21(2):167-75

11-Agnihotri S, Vaidya AD. A novel

approach to study antibacterial properties of volatile components of selected Indian medicinal herbs. Indian J Exp Biol 1996 Jul;34(7):712-5

12-Aruna K, Sivaramakrishnan VM. Anticarcinogenic effects of some Indian plant products. Food Chem Toxicol 1992 Nov;30(11):953-6 12a-Ota M, Shimizu Y, Tonosaki K, Ariyoshi Y. Synthesis, characterization, and sweetness-suppressing activities of gurmarin analogues missing one disulfide bond. Biopolymers 1998 Aug;46(2):65-73

12b-Arai K, Ishima R, Morikawa S, Miyasaka A, Imoto T, Yoshimura S, Aimoto S, Akasaka K. Three-dimensional structure of gurmarin, a sweet taste- suppressing polypeptide. J Biomol NMR 1995 Apr;5(3):297-305

13-Dwivedi S, Agarwal MP. Antianginal

and cardioprotective effects of Terminalia arjuna, an indigenous drug, in coronary artery disease. J Assoc Physicians India 1994 Apr;42(4):287-9

13a-Bharani A, Ganguly A, Bhargava KD. Salutary effect of Terminalia Arjuna in patients with severe refractory heart failure. Int J Cardiol 1995 May;49(3):191-9 13b-Pettit GR, Hoard MS, Doubek DL, Schmidt JM, Pettit RK, Tackett LP, Chapuis JC. Antineoplastic agents 338. The cancer cell growth inhibitory. Constituents of Terminalia arjuna (Combretaceae). J Ethnopharmacol 1996 Aug;53(2):57-63

13c-Dwivedi S, Jauhari R. Beneficial effects of Terminalia arjuna in coronary artery disease. Indian Heart J 1997 Sep-Oct;49(5):507-10 13d-Seth SD, Maulik M, Katiyar CK, Maulik SK. Role of Lipistat in protection against isoproterenol induced myocardial necrosis in rats: a biochemical and histopathological study. Indian J Physiol Pharmacol 1998 Jan;42(1):101-6

14-Atal CK, Zutshi U, Rao PG. Scientific evidence on the role of Ayurvedic herbals on bioavailability of drugs. J Ethnopharmacol 1981 Sep;4(2):229-32 15-Perez C, Anesini C. Antibacterial activity of alimentary plants against Staphylococcus aureus growth. Am J Chin Med 1994;22(2):169-74

15a-Nakatani N, Inatani R, Ohta H, Nishioka A. Chemical constituents of peppers (Piper spp.) and application to food preservation: naturally occurring antioxidative compounds. Environ Health Perspect 1986 Aug;67:135-42

16-Rana BK, Singh UP, Taneja V. Antifungal activity and kinetics of inhibition by essential oil isolated from leaves of Aegle marmelos. J Ethnopharmacol 1997 Jun;57(1):29-34 17-Nayak AK, Karnad DR,

Abraham P , Mistry FP . Metronidazole relieves symptoms in irritable bowel syndrome: the confusion with so-called 'chronic amebiasis'. Indian J Gastroenterol 1997 Oct;16(4):137-9

18-Kaufman PB, Duke JA, Brielmann H, Boik J, Hoyt JE. A comparative survey of leguminous plants as sources of the isoflavones, genistein and daidzein: implications for human nutrition and health. J Altern Complement Med 1997 Spring;3(1):7-12

18a-Fu JX. [Measurement of MEFV in 66 cases of asthma in the convalescent stage and after treatment with Chinese herbs]. Chung Hsi I Chieh Ho Tsa Chih 1989 Nov;9(11):658-9, 644

19-Verma SK, et al. Effect of Commiphora mukul (gum guggulu) in patients of hyperlipidemia with special reference to

HDL-cholesterol. Indian J Med Res. 1988 Apr;87:356-60.

19a-Singh RB, Niaz MA, Ghosh S. Hypolipidemic and antioxidant effects of Commiphora mukul as an adjunct to dietary therapy in patients with hypercholesterolemia. Cardiovasc Drugs Ther 1994 Aug;8(4):659-64

20-Hussain MS, Chandrasekhara N. Effect on curcumin on cholesterol gall-stone induction in mice. Indian J Med Res 96:288-291; 1992. 20a-Srivastava R, Srimal RC. Modification of certain inflammation-induced biochemical changes by curcumin. Indian J Med Res 81:215-223; 1985.

20b-Nagabhushan M, Bhide SV. Curcumin as an inhibitor of cancer. J Am Coll Nutr 11:192-198; 1992. 20c-Kuttan R, Sudheeran PC, Josph CD. Turmeric and curcumin as topical agents in cancer therapy.

Tumori (ITALY) 73:29-31; 1987.

20d-Retardation of experimental tumorigenesis and reduction in DNA adducts by turmeric and curcumin. Krishnaswamy K, Goud VK, Sesikeran B, et al. Nutr Cancer 1998;30:163-166.

21-Miller AL. Botanical influences on cardiovascular disease. Altern Med Rev 1998 Dec;3(6):422-431 22-Natarajan S, Paily PP. Effect of topical Hydrocotyle Asiatica in psoriasis.

Indian J Dermatol 1973 Jul;18(4):82-5 22a-Tripathi YB, Chaurasia S, Tripathi E, Upadhyay A, Dubey GP. Bacopa monniera Linn. as an antioxidant: mechanism of action. Indian J Exp Biol 1996 Jun;34(6):523-6

22b-Parikh MD, Pradhan, PV, Shah LP, Bagadia Vn. Evaluation of Indigenous

Psychototropic Drugs- A Preliminary Study. Journ. Res. Ay. Sid. Vol 5; no. 1-4 1984 23- Phadke SA, Kulkarni SD. Screening of in vitro antibacterial activity of Terminalia chebula, Eclipta alba and Ocimum sanctum. Indian J Med Sci 1989 May;43(5):113-7

24-el-Mekkawy S, Meselhy MR, Kusumoto IT, Kadota S, Hattori M, Namba T. Inhibitory effects of Egyptian folk medicines on human immuno-deficiency virus (HIV) reverse transcriptase. Chem Pharm Bull (Tokyo) 1995 Apr;43(4):641-8

24a-Ahmad I, Mehmood Z, Mohammad F. Screening of some Indian medicinal plants for their anti-microbial properties. J Ethnopharmacol 1998 Sep;62(2):183-93 25- Sohni YR, Bhatt RM.

Activity of a crude extract formulation in experimental hepatic amoebiasis and in immuno-modulation studies. J

Ethnopharmacol 1996 Nov;54(2-3):119-24 25a-Rawat AK, Mehrotra S, Tripathi SC, Shome U. Hepatoprotective activity of Boerhaavia diffusa L. roots--a popular Indian ethnomedicine. J Ethnopharmacol 1997 Mar;56(1):61-6

25b-Deshpande PJ, Singh R, Bhatt NS, Clinical Efefct of an Ayurvedic Drug L2002 on Hepatobiliary Disorders. Journal of NIMA, Dec 1994 26-Thatte UM, Rao SG, Dahanukar SA. Tinospora cordifolia induces colony stimulating activity in serum. J Postgrad Med 1994 Oct-Dec;40(4):202-3

26a-Nagarkatti DS, Rege NN, Desai NK, Dahanukar SA. Modulation of Kupffer cell activity by Tinospora cordifolia in liver damage. J Postgrad Med 1994 Apr-Jun;40(2):65-7 26b-Rege N, Bapat RD, Koti R, Desai NK, Dahanukar S. Immunotherapy with Tinospora cordifolia: a new lead in the management of obstructive jaundice. Indian J Gastroenterol 1993 Jan;12(1):5-8

26c-Deshpande PD, Singh R, Bhatt NS, Clinical Trial of Ayturvedic Drug U-144 (K-4 Tablets) in Urinary Tract 85

Infections. The Medicine & Surgery. Vol 32; no. 10/11. Oct - Nov 1944 27-Baskaran K, Kizar Ahamath B, Radha Shanmugasundaram K, Shanmugasundaram ER. Antidiabetic effect of a leaf extract from Gymnema sylvestre in non-insulin- dependent diabetes mellitus patients. J Ethnopharmacol 1990 Oct;30(3):295-300 27a-Pal KNC. Effects of a Herbomineral Compound on Diabetes. Ayurved Samachar: Issue 8; vol 10 2 Feb. 1988 28-Goel RK, Banerjee RS, Acharya SB. Antiulcerogenic and anti-inflammatory studies with shilajit. J Ethnopharmacol 1990 Apr;29(1):95-103

29-Noor H, Ashcroft SJ. Pharmacological characterization of the anti-hyperglycemic properties of Tinospora crispa extract. J Ethnopharmacol 1998 Aug;62(1):7-13 30-Qian-Cutrone J, Huang S, Trimble J, Li H, Lin PF, Alam M, Klohr SE, Kadow KF. Niruriside, a new HIV REV/RRE binding inhibitor from Phyllanthus niruri. J Nat Prod 1996 Feb;59(2):196-9

30a-Ogata T, Higuchi H, Mochida S, Matsumoto H, Kato A, Endo T, Kaji A, Kaji H. HIV-1 reverse transcriptase inhibitor from Phyllanthus niruri. AIDS Res Hum Retroviruses 1992 Nov;8(11):1937-44

31-Mehrotra R, Rawat S, Kulshreshtha DK, Patnaik GK, Dhawan BN In vitro studies on the effect of certain natural products against hepatitis B virus. Indian J Med Res 1990 Apr;92:133-8

32-Alarcon-Aguilara FJ, Roman-Ramos R,

Perez-Gutierrez S, Aguilar-Contreras A, Contreras-Weber CC, Flores-Saenz JL. Study of the anti-hyperglycemic effect of plants used as anti-diabetics. J Ethnopharmacol 1998 Jun;61(2):101-10 33-Akhtar MS, Qureshi AQ, Iqbal J. Antidiabetic evaluation of Mucuna pruriens, Linn seeds.

JPMA J Pak Med Assoc 1990 Jul;40(7):147-50 34-Chithra P, Sajithlal GB, Chandrakasan G. Influence of Aloe vera on collagen turnover in healing of dermal wounds in rats. Indian J Exp Biol 1998 Sep;36(9):896-901

34a- ez B, Avila G, Segura D, Escalante B. Anti- inflammatory activity of extracts from Aloe vera gel. J Ethnopharmacol 1996 Dec;55(1):69-75 35-Nair SC, Pannikar B, Panikkar KR. Anti-tumour activity of saffron (Crocus sativus). Cancer Lett 1991 May 1;57(2):109-14

36-Nalini N, Sabitha K, Viswanathan P, Menon VP. Influence of spices on the bacterial (enzyme) activity in experimental colon cancer. 37-Duwiejua M, Zeitlin IJ, Waterman PG, Chapman J, Mhango GJ, Provan GJ. Anti-inflammatory activity of resins from some species of the plant family Burseraceae. Planta Med 1993 Feb;59(1):12-6

38-Chiang HC, Tseng TH, Wang CJ, Chen CF, Kan WS. Experimental anti-tumor agents from Solanum indicum L. Anticancer Res 1991 Sep-Oct;11(5):1911-7 39-Ammon HP, Wahl MA. Pharmacology of Curcuma longa. Planta Med 1991 Feb;57(1):1-7.

40-Srivastava KC. Extracts from two frequently consumed spices--cumin (Cuminum cyminum) and turmeric (Curcuma longa)--inhibit platelet aggregation and alter eicosanoid biosynthesis in human blood platelets. Prostaglandins Leukot Essent Fatty Acids 1989 Jul;37(1):57-64.

41-Bone ME, Wilkinson DJ, Young JR, McNeil J, Charlton S. Ginger Root- a New Anti-emetic. The Effect of Ginger Root on Postoperative Nausea and Vomiting after Major Gynaecological Surgery. Anesthesia 45:8, 1980 Aug. 669- 71

41a-Srivastava KC, Mustafa T. Ginger in Rheumatism and Musculoskeletal Disorders. Med Hypothesis 39:4, 1992 Dec. 342-8 41b-Grontvend A, Brask T, Kambskard J, Hentzer E. Ginger Root Against Seasickness. A Controlled Trial on the Open Sea. Acta Otolaryngology (Stockh) 105:1-2, 1988 Jan-Feb 45-9

41c-Thakur M, Bhatt NS, Mishra S, et. al. Effects of Ayurvedic Drug (AB + R) in Indigestion. Medicine & Surgery. May -

August 1996/23 .42-Li W, Asada Y, Yoshikawa T. Anti-microbial flavonids from Glycyrrhiza glabra hairy root cultures. Planta Med. 1998 Dec; 64 (8): 746-7

42a-Belinky PA, Aviram M, Fuhrman B, Rosenblat M, Vaya J. The anti-oxidative effects of the isoflavan glabridin on endogenous constituents of LDL during its oxidation. Atherosclerosis 1988. Mar; 137 (1): 49-61

42b-Badam L. In vitro antiviral activity of indigenous glycyrrhizin, licorice and glycyrrhizic acid (sigma) on Japanese encephalitis virus. J. Comun. Dis. 1997 June; 29(2): 91-9

Summary

More than 2,000 scientific studies on Ayurvedic herbs have found them to be effective in healing various diseases, and without causing side effects. The cost of individual herbs, or herbal combinations, are extremely inexpensive compared to allopathic drugs used for the same treatments. With scientific proof of efficacy and cost effectiveness studies in hand, modern health care can integrate Ayurvedic medicine into its practice and save a fortune in health care costs.

Chapter 12 Frequently Asked Questions

Below are some of the most common questions asked at our center over the decades.

General

Is Ayurveda covered by Medical Insurance?

At the time of publishing this book most of the HMOs are considering covering various forms of alternative medicine including yoga, acupuncture, and chiropractic. Since Ayurveda is relatively new in the US no formal licensing or national certification is available. Some of the HMOs have said they will therefore consider individual Ayurvedic practitioners on a case by case basis.

How do you know when to consult a medical doctor or an Ayurvedic practitioner?

Any serious or possible life threatening conditions absolutely require visiting a licensed medical professional. It is also advisable to check most health conditions with doctors. If they say no serious complications can develop you can choose to follow Ayurvedic therapies. For simple conditions that do not require a doctor's visit (e.g., a cold), obviously one can directly visit the Ayurvedic practitioner.

Do I need to receive regular health checkups if I am following an Ayurvedic program?

It is always wise to receive regular checkups. Western medicine can confirm the condition of your health. Cholesterol, blood pressure, heart testing, etc. will put your mind at ease and validate the results of your Ayurvedic therapies. Ayurveda compliments the modern medical practice; it doesn't replace it.

My doctor is close-minded to any alternative medicine. What should I do?

Many qualified and respected medical professionals are open to alternative therapies. In fact, more and more medical professionals are becoming receptive to such complimentary therapies. Respected news and radio programs, newspapers, and magazines are reporting on the benefits of such alternative care. Many respected medical professionals are speaking on TV, radio and in the print media about the value of holistic care. Even the HMOs are preparing to cover alternative medicine.

There is no harm in finding another qualified medical professional that is willing to work with your wishes to use alternative care along with Western medical observation and possible treatment. On the other hand, by limiting your healing options only to Western medicine, one is left with the possibilities of expensive treatments, side effects and the inability to heal a certain condition. Professionals need to respect the intuition and feelings of their clients.

My holistic practitioner advises me against visiting medical doctors. Should I listen to them?

Ayurveda believes there is a time and place for all things. If a person develops appendicitis, it is too late for holistic measures; it's time for surgery. At the same time, if you can use some simple natural therapies to heal non- emergency conditions, and for preventing illness without side effects, it is better than risking expensive therapies and side effects.

It is a good rule of thumb for any professional, holistic or modern medical, to have an open mind and be willing to listen to their client's intuitions and feelings. It is better to find a holistic practitioner who views their relationship with modern medical professionals as complimentary rather than adversarial.

If Ayurveda is so useful why don't doctors know about Ayurveda and other holistic therapies?

Simply, Western medical professionals have only been trained in drugs and surgery. Only recently have some medical schools begun initial training in alternative therapies such as holistic nutrition, prevention, hands-on healing etc. Often these courses are still optional.

Many top medical colleges are investigating Ayurveda and holistic health. Harvard sponsors an alternative health symposium. Columbia University has Ayurvedic symposiums several times a year.

My doctor says they cannot do anything for my condition. Can Ayurveda help?

Ayurveda looks at the whole person, looks to the cause of illness and sees four levels of disease development unavailable to modern technology. At the very least, Ayurveda can help one improve their general health and well-being. Further, Ayurveda has had success in healing many diseases where modern medicine has no answers.

I have read about Ayurvedic doctors and Ayurvedic practitioners. What is the difference?

Three types of Ayurvedic professionals exist.

1. The true Ayurvedic doctor is one who has studied Ayurveda in India. Legally they are not allowed to be called doctors in the US

because they have not received medical certification in the US. However, they have been trained in both Ayurvedic and Western medicine and can converse equally well in either language.

2. The medical doctor who has studied Ayurveda in the US. The extent of their Ayurvedic knowledge depends upon the quality of their training. Just because they are licensed medical doctors doesn't automatically guarantee they offer better Ayurvedic services. On the other hand, medical doctors properly trained in Ayurveda are better able to speak both languages. Some clients are more comfortable speaking the language of modern medicine.

3. The Ayurvedic practitioner has no medical license but has received Ayurvedic training in the US. Again, the quality of their training determines their abilities. They may

be more or less qualified than a medical doctor trained in Ayurveda who also was Ayurvedically trained in the US. The main drawback is they may not be able to speak the language of modern medicine. This only presents a language problem to those who insist on hearing things in medical terminology.

Which is better, Ayurveda or Western medicine?

It is not a matter of, which is better. The more accurate question is when is the time to use one approach or the other. As discussed earlier, it is better to view these sciences as complimentary instead of adversarial. A practical rule of thumb is use natural methods wherever and whenever possible, but always use modern medicine to monitor one's health. In this way, medical doctors will not be over burdened with clients they don't need to treat; they will have more time to care for the truly needy.

Why can't I just treat my health symptoms? Why do I need to follow an entire holistic routine?

If a person removes the surface symptoms without eradicating the root cause, the original symptoms will return. It is not enough to look at isolated parts of one's health. All areas of life affect the other areas. Sometimes lifestyle changes are required to stop the imbalancing of one's health condition.

We have been brought up to expect medicine to offer a magic cure. When people start holistic therapies often they still keep this idea in mind. Even in holistic approaches, no magic bullet exists. Persons must look at all areas of life to see what is the cause of the disorder. Lifestyle changes may be required. One cannot expect to continue following harmful habits without suffering the consequences.

The value of Ayurveda is that it offers an understanding and ability to take control over one's own health. A great deal of self-worth and peace of mind develops when one takes responsibility for their health and finds they are in control. But with knowledge comes responsibility. It is not enough to know something intellectually. Persons must live according to their health requirements in order to reap health benefits.

Herbs

Are Ayurvedic herbs safe to take?

Generally, yes. It is advisable to use herbal companies or Ayurvedic practitioners that have a good reputation. Ask for references if you wish. Best of all, use products that a family member or friend has already found effective.

Some herbs do have side effects if taken by certain people or at certain times. It is best to read about the herbs first and to consult with a qualified Ayurvedic practitioner before taking any unknown herbs or using any unknown herb company.

How long do I have to take the herbs?

For mild conditions like a cold, herbs are taken until the symptoms completely disappear. More chronic conditions require six months to one year to heal, and also to build healthy cells and tissues, and replenish the immune system.

Traditional Ayurveda says that people with hereditary conditions or those born with a health disorder need to use herbs for life. Ayurveda says these conditions need to be kept in check or else they will quickly return. In these cases, people will be able to live normal, healthy lives, but need to take the herbs. For these people herbs need to be thought of as food supplements. No one complains that they have to eat, drink and breathe air every day for the rest of their lives. Herbs need to be thought of in the same light.

In the 21st century science has discovered that hereditary is only determines around 20% of the likelihood we will have the same health issue as our relatives. With proper lifestyle and changing our brainwaves and limited thoughts through neuroscience, meditation etc. avoiding and healing hereditary conditions are more likely. Therefore, I feel we will discover in the near future that herbs may not be a lifetime requirement for hereditary conditions — just a heads up to the future of energy medicine.

What herb dose should I take?

Herb doses depend on several factors, strength, age, *dosha*, severity of the disease etc. It is best to ask your Ayurvedic practitioner for your recommended doses.

Is it safe to take Ayurvedic herbs while taking my prescription medication or going for surgery?

Generally, no side effects will occur, but research which herbs are not advised. Also, since one is using a double-barrel approach to healing a condition, it is advised to monitor your health levels more frequently. The use of both medicines may cause quicker normalizing of levels. The medical doctor needs to be advised of this so they can reduce the doses of the medication.

Can I take herbs instead of medication?

This is only a good idea for non-life-threatening situations. Consult with both the doctor and Ayurvedic practitioner; it is not advisable to make this decision on one's own.

What's the difference between isolated extracts of herbs and whole herbs?

There are now TV commercials proudly stating that because their herbal products have isolated herbal extracts, active ingredient levels are guaranteed, so you know that the quality and safety is guaranteed. The reality is that once you take active ingredients from a herb, you have a drug (i.e., this is how many medicines are prepared) with many side effects.

Once you tamper with Mother Nature's herb and extract one active ingredient, you change the entire property of the product—its effects and side effects are now unknown. Mother Nature adds many ingredients in a herb. Some will counter the side effects of another ingredient. Whenever mankind plays God and thinks it can outsmart nature, trouble ensues.

So, Ayurveda suggests it safer to take whole herbs from reputable companies. Guaranteed levels are not as important as holistic quality herbs.

Meditation

I cannot meditate. How do I keep thoughts out of my mind?

This is a misconception. Meditation is a natural situation. Forcing thoughts out of the mind is not natural; forcing anything is not natural. Meditation has many forms. Prayer, contemplation, and mantras are forms most commonly associated with meditation.

In some cases, art, music, or just doing what you love connects one with the Divine. For others, active meditation is more suitable such as helping others, religious ceremonies, rituals, and chanting. The key is that each individual finds what best suits their temperament. Whatever is natural will bring a sense of mental peace and eventually Divine bliss.

Do I have to change religions to meditate?
No, whatever forms of meditation or prayer are appealing is what will work best for each person. There is no best religion; there is no best form of meditation.

Organized religion does not work for me. Is there another definition of spirituality?

Yes, each person was created by God and has the Divine spark within them. Each person can find his or her own inner path back to God. Whatever brings peace of mind is spiritual. Helping others, being ethical, finding a purpose in life, all these are ways to develop one's spirituality.

Is the peace that comes from meditation make one become a zombie?

Just the opposite. Brain washing or the zombie-state is one of complete loss of one's mental control. Someone else is controlling the mind.

Meditation frees the mind from stress and ideas that enslave it. The mind has more clarity, awareness, and penetrative abilities. Thus, it can't be taken over in stressful situations; the mind remains clear, calm and alert.

Yoga

What is the value of yoga?

The benefits of yoga are many. Yoga postures keep the body loose and toned. Mind/body coordination is improved. Organs are toned, health concerns are healed; memory, concentration and peace of mind are developed.

Yoga seems too hard. How can I ever get into postures I see others do?

Yoga is another natural, gentle healing process. It is a method to quiet one's mind, bringing one's awareness within. The idea of competition, doing as good or better than the person next to you is not the goal of yoga. The goal of yoga is to feel at peace with oneself, not to compare oneself to others. Each person is unique; each reflects a unique Divine quality.

Whatever extent one can reach in any posture, they should feel at home with themselves. Ayurveda says the goal of life is Self-Realization. This means one realizes they are eternal, Divine. If one is eternal, they only have to realize this through experience. Each person is already eternal, they needn't do anything other than realize this.

One can be Self-Realized and not be able to perfect a yoga pose. So, the focus is on that peace of mind which, in that quietude, allows one to realize their true nature; anxiety or impatience over not perfecting a pose only agitates the mind and delays Self-Realization.

Some people are naturally more flexible; it's in their genes. They can perfect a pose in a short time. Others may never perfect a pose. The purpose of yoga is to prepare one for Self-Realization; for most people, it is not a sole path to the soul's liberation

Exercise

If I eat right and take herbs, do I have to exercise?

Exercise is important for many reasons. Mind and body coordination is enhanced, toxins are cleansed, circulation is improved, mental stresses are reduced, and depression, anxiety and anger are reduced. Some sort of aerobic exercise is very important as part of one's holistic health lifestyle. Walking for even 1/2 hour, three times a week will result in noticeable positive changes in one's physical and mental health. One's spirit and vitality will be enhanced.

Nutrition

Will taking herbs be sufficient to heal my condition?

Herbs will help restore balance, but if one continually eats foods that lack nutrition or create an elemental imbalance, health will never achieve maximum potential. Aspirins will take away a headache but if one keeps hitting their head against the wall, even the aspirin will not prevent the headache. Herbs are best viewed as food supplements. Fresh, organic foods eaten in season will offer the best form of overall nutrition. Eating foods that balance one's *dosha* will work more subtly to achieve balance.

Self-Realization

I cannot grasp the concept of Self-Realization. Will this cause delays in my spiritual development?

The only ones who completely grasp Self-Realization are those who have realized the true nature of their soul. Until then it is only an idea in the mind, not an actual experience. Analogies can be given to gain a hint of this reality but not until one experiences this eternal condition will one fully grasp it.

The state of eternity is unbounded, beyond form, beyond words, beyond the realm that senses experience. Therefore, how can one adequately describe or experience that which cannot be explained or experienced? When the individual, thinking as an individual, expands and merges into their eternal Self, a state of one-ness with all things becomes reality. When a drop of water falls into the ocean, it loses its individual status and becomes a part of the entire ocean.

The raindrop can say I am the ocean. One cannot distinguish between the drop and the ocean. This is an illustration of how one merges with their eternal soul upon Self-Realization.

The path of realization is a gradual one; it is not like an on off switch. A person is not at one level of individuality for years or lifetimes and then suddenly becomes Self-

Realized. A gradual culturing of one's mind, heart and soul develops over time.

The process is gradual and natural. The Self-Realized person will not look, act, or talk differently than others. Only their internal perception of life will be different. They will see all people, animals, plants, etc. as a part of the Divine eternal ocean rather than separate, individual drops. All of life will be delicate and Divine. This quiet appreciation is carried within, not readily observed by others.

Many people read about Self-Realization and have some intellectual understanding of this state. They have been studying books and spiritual practices for so long their egos may begin to boast that they know what Self-Realization is. But the soul is beyond thoughts of the mind. A parrot can be taught to say the phrase, 'I am eternal' but this does not make the parrot Self-Realized. If a cat comes along to eat the parrot, the bird resorts to its natural state and squawks in fear of its life. People may try to impress others with their intellectual grasp of spirituality, but this merely reflects their egos, not their soul.

The *Vedic* texts say the Self-Realized person avoids the spotlight, not wanting attention heaped upon them. They prefer the peace of the Divine not to be pestered by the inquisitive. The Buddhists say that before Self-Realization a person may be seen to chop wood and carry water. After Self-Realization, this person will be seen chopping wood and carrying water. The only thing that changes is one's inner peace and bliss upon contact with the Divine.

Therefore, there is no need to be discouraged if one does not grasp the idea of Self-Realization. It is more important to take care of one's health, work in a purposeful career, and to develop one's spirituality. It is better to contribute something to one's community, leaving it a better place than what one found.

Be virtuous and ethical. Cultivate forgiveness and openness to all people and all beliefs. Harbor no hatred; this clouds the heart and mind and delays one's Self-development. These are the actions of the Self- Realized. One can be grateful to be able to follow these actions. These actions cultivate Self-Realization. Over time explanations of Self-Realization will become more and more appreciated.

Afterword

A 2-Decade Review

It has been nearly 20 years since I first prepared this book for my Ayurveda certification students, and now with the digital publishing technology I have decided to reprint and share the book with everyone. In the process, I made a few minor changes to the book.

It also feels appropriate to update the evolution of my healing lifestyle & career as it seems to have been a lifetime ago when this book was printed.

From my first experiences with Ayurveda back in 1988, I loved two things about it; it worked quickly - in some cases instantly, and often within three days; and I loved the nurturing style Ayurveda offers (i.e., it nourishes what is missing instead of attacking the excess) thereby gently balancing and loving the body, mind, and spirit.

Then in 2010 I found myself visiting the Amazon rainforest where two shamans told me I was a natural born shaman and healer. During a ceremony, a spirit descended and blew into my heart and instantly I felt cleared (I'm not sure exactly cleared of what). I realized I could do this for others and when I returned home I began experimenting with shamanic energy healing, which I called 'instant healing through the heart' and I found a quicker, more profound level of healing occurring.

Ayurveda became a lifestyle for me, foods, yoga, nature etc. But the need for herbs and other 'therapies' became less—I could just do some energy work on myself and was cleared on deeper levels.

For any Ayurvedic purists who believe Ayurveda is all you need, I respect your views. However, in my quest to help people as quickly and profoundly (i.e. spiritually) as possible, shamanic energy medicine has become my natural healing, prevention, and rejuvenation method.

Along with shamanic energy medicine, I also became aware of people's mental outlook impacts their physical health, relationships, and even career. In Patanjali's Yoga Sutras, a wonderful Vedic text, he basically says there are two types of thoughts we thing; harmonious and discordant. And I found the more harmonious thoughts we think we healthier and happier we are and the more we grow in life. Conversely, the more we tell ourselves limiting beliefs like, I'm not worthy, I can't do that, etc. the more that becomes our reality.

And so, another investigation into how to instantly dispel limiting beliefs led me to study EEG neuroscience brainwaves (i.e., listening to alpha, theta, etc. mp3s), studying hypnotism and NLP (neuro-linguistic programming), and also testing out cold lasers. All these have helped me and my clients achieve transformations in minutes rather than days, weeks, or even decades.

For example, I had a person with a back injury who was seeing a holistic practitioner (chiropractor, acupuncturist, etc. — I don't remember the healing modality) for about ten years. She only stopped seeing them because they passed away. As I started my energy work with NLP and cold laser, she felt the back pain shift within five minutes. Miracle! I said if the pain shifted, it can't be a physical issue or else it wouldn't shift. In the next five minutes the pain vanished! I love it!

While it may seem like I strayed from Ayurveda, in reality my path is healing as fast and as deeply as possible. So, where Ayurveda helps—like with food plans, I use it. When I can help someone more quickly with energy work, I use that. I am less concerned with the tool as the person's healing.

The most recent level of healing I have developed was my life-long psychic mediumship. Ok I hear some of you rolling your eyes. I didn't believe in it most of my young life — even though I had dreams predicting my future since around age 10 — and they ultimately came true at age 18. The predictions were for an unpleasant outcome that did happen, so I never thought these visions were 'gifts'; more like curses. It was only through using Ayurveda and Vedic Astrology that I found a way to help people when I had psychic (intuitive) insights for them. I just never said I was using these gifts because it might freak folks out. The word 'psychic' has gotten such a bad rap — and in many cases deservedly so.

But last year spirit invited me to go deeper with these gifts and I became more myself, more natural as a person who talks with loved ones who have passed, angels, and guides and masters. Instead of filling my brain to remember things others have taught me, I have direct contact with wise souls and those with knowledge of things I do not have.

This leaves my heart open to just feeling connected with all of life - including life after life; nothing dies. And when loves ones or spirit guides tell you things that come true, or tell you very specific things about a adult client's childhood (e.g., the color pattern of their grandmother's apron; their favorite game) that they confirm, there is a scientific proof method confirming there is a greater knowledge out there than just my brain.

So, plugging into universal spirit or cosmic wisdom is the most amazing part of my life to date. Feeling connected to nature as I see and speak with shaman spirits, angels, my own ancestors and my guru is the most alive and complete I have ever been.

Since writing this book in 2000, we reached 2012 which is said to mean we have as a planet chosen to not destroy ourselves with a final war, and that we are now on the way to evolve into higher spiritual beings. In a sense, the old world did end. The limits of what we were taught, including some spiritual lessons are no longer valid.

It is up to us to be open to new information that each and every one of us can connect to by going within, asking and listening. Some of my lifelong visions are just beginning to come true. One such vision was that we can live a very long time — hundreds of years — like the prophets of our ancestors.

But best of all for me is that we are evolving into a compassionate, joyful human race where wellness, equality, abundance, wisdom, and joy is quietly but surely developing on the planet. If you look for it and don't doubt it, you will experience it.

Better still, you can create it. Science tells us if we are feeling down and fake a smile, a signal is sent to our brain that we are smiling and it begins to secret 'happy hormones' and our body does begin to start feeling better.

Neuroscience, Quantum Physics, & Metaphysics are all saying the same thing — that humans, nature, and everything is, at our essence, spirit. We are all one-connected.

Choose your vision of what your paradise looks like and compassionately and joyfully dance your way into that life. You will feel closer to it more and more.

Ayurveda can be defined as anything that brings health, and that covers all forms of healing. Based on that, welcome to the new improved Ayurveda 2.0

Live well my friends

Glossary

6 stages of disease development method to identify cause and stages of disorders

Abhyanga special Ayurvedic massage practices

Agni digestive fire (enzymes)

Ali Akbar Khan world renown classical Indian musician

Alternative medicine non-drug-based healing approaches

Ama undigested food toxins

Aromatherapy therapeutic use of scents

Ayurveda India's 5,000-year-old holistic

science of life

Basti medicated enema

Charak Samhita One of the three main original Ayurvedic texts

Color therapy therapeutic use of colors

Complimentary medicine see alternative medicine

Dharma life purpose or mission

Dosha personal constitution

Elements essential fundamentals in all people, animals, and nature

Energetics underlying forces of health

Feng Shui Chinese architectural placement

Ghee clarified butter

Health balanced state of the *doshas* and elements

Herbology medicinal use of herbs

Himalayas mountain range in India

Holistic health see alternative medicine

Jaggery Indian cane sugar

Jyotish Indian or Vedic Astrology

Kapha phlegm; constitution or humor; water/earth energetic

Ketu south node of the Moon used in Jyotish astrology

Kundalini Shakti inner spiritual energy force

Lassi yogurt/water drink

Mantra healing vibrations or names of God for Self- Realization

Meditation various methods for peace and Self-Realization

Music therapy therapeutic use of music

Nasya medicated nasal therapies

Ojas life sap—the essence of immune system and spiritual energy

Origin Sites where the three *doshas* begin to cause illness

Pancha karma five procedures to rid the body of toxins

Paneer homemade cheese

Pitta bile; a constitution or humor; fire energetic

Prakrti a person's life-long constitutional

nature (see *dosha*)

Pulse analysis methods to learn one's constitution and imbalance

Rahu north node of the Moon in Jyotish astrology

Rakta moksha therapeutic blood letting

Ravi Shankar world renown classical Indian musician

Root-cause the underlying or core reason a disease appears

Sattwa purity

Self-Realization the goal of life—mental peace and bliss are ever present. One realizes their true eternal nature.

Shakti (see kundalini)

Shiro Dhara therapeutic warm oil flow to

the head

Tridosha a constitution involving all three *doshas*

Vikrti the current state of one's health or balance

Vamana therapeutic vomiting to release excess Kapha

Vastu Shastra (Vedic Architecture) laws of nature harmonizing structures with the earth, planets and persons' health

Vata wind; constitution or humor; ether/air element (traditional word for Vata)

Vata another name for Vata

Vedas India's ancient Hindu scriptures (religion and science covering all areas of life.

Virechana therapeutic purgatives to release excess Pitta

Yoga gentle stretching poses

Self-Education

Ayurveda Encyclopedia by Swami Sada Shiva Tirtha
https://swamisadashivatirtha.com/enlighten/books/

Yoga Vani: Instructions for the Attainment of Siddhayoga by Swami Shankar Purushottam Tirtha
https://swamisadashivatirtha.com/contact-swamiji-orange-cowboy/

Guru Bani: 100 Ways to Attain Peace by Swami Shankar Purushottam Tirtha
https://swamisadashivatirtha.com/contact-swamiji-orange-cowboy/

About the Author

Swami Sadashiva Tirtha, D.Sc. - Bio
1974 Swamiji was initiated into formal meditation & yoga from India
1975 BA in Interdisciplinary Studies
1976 became a TM meditation teacher
1980 MA in Nonverbal Communication Research
1988 Met his guru in India
   Advanced private study with BHU Ayurveda professors in India
1989 Ayurveda Certification
   Founded monastery in US offering spiritual & Ayurveda support
1990 Published *Yoga Vani* by Swami Shankar Purushottam Tirtha

Advanced study with Ayurvedic doctors in Himalayas

Developed one of the first Ayurveda herbal product lines in USA

1991 Founded International Vedic Institute [one of the first Ayurveda schools in the USA]

Advanced study with Ayurvedic doctors in Himalayas

Recognized as swami from his guru, Swami Narayan Tirtha

1995 Published second book, Guru Bani by same author

1998 Wrote the Ayurveda Encyclopedia (30,000 copies in print to date)

Completed Ayurveda scientific research study on allergies

1999 Earned first Doctor of Science (D.Sc.) in Ayurveda medicine (first Ayurveda D.Sc. the USA)

2000 Research study published in American Ayurveda Journal (July)

Wrote the Ayurveda Primer ebook

2007 Wrote Bhagavad Gita for Modern Times (commentary/ translation)

2010 Met with shaman in Ecuador's Amazon rainforest who recognized Swamiji as a natural-born shaman & healer
International Joy Workshops

2011 Developed Instant Energy & Healing through the Heart Meditation course

2012-2014 Co-chair Spiritual Arts festival
Created Medical IntuitionTraining/ Certification Course

2015-Present Stress Management Workshops at Colleges & Companies

2016 Advanced Mediumship studies at Lily Daly, NY. Earned Certified Advanced Psychic Medium title through Lisa Williams International School of Spiritual Development

2017 Wrote the book, 21 Days of Joy: Embracing Our Essential Nature
New Courses: Meditation for Beginners; Shaman Training
Published Ayurveda Primer (previously only available for Swamiji's Ayurveda certification students)

Miscellaneous
Speaker:

White House Commission on Complementary & Alternative Medicine Policy
John Hopkins University
Penn State University
St. George's Medical College, Grenada
Ayurveda College Haridwar, India
Toastmasters ACG, ALB

Authored an Amazon #1 Bestseller, The Ayurveda Encyclopedia (30000+ copies in print)

Websites:
http://SwamiSadashivaTirtha.com
http://TheHipGuru.com
Ashram: http://SwamiNarayanTirtha.org

Facebook: https://facebook.com/monkmedium

Radio Host:
http://www.blogtalkradio.com/cowboyswamishaman

Youtube: https://www.youtube.com/user/TheHipGurusGuide/

Bibliography

Adwankar MK; Chitnis MP. In Vivo Anticancer Activity of RC-18: a Plant Isolate from Rubia Cordifolia, Linn. Against a Spectrum of Experimental Tumour Models. Chemotherapy, 28: 4, 1982, 291-3

Agnihotri S, Vaidya AD. A novel approach to study antibacterial properties of volatile components of selected Indian medicinal herbs. Indian J Exp Biol 1996 Jul;34(7):712-715

Badmaev V, Majeed M. Effects of Ayurvedic Herbs. Health Supplement Retailer Magazine. November 1995

Badmaev V, Majeed M. *Ayurvedic Adaptogens and Bioprotectants*. Natural Food Merchandiser's Nutrition Science News Magazine. September 1995

Baskaran K; Kizar Ahamath B; Radha

Shanmugasundaram K; Shanmugasundaram ER. Antidiabetic Effect of a Leaf Extract from Gymnema Sylvestre in Non-insulin Dependent diabetes mellitus patients. J Ethnopharmacol, 30: 3, 1990 Oct, 295-300

Bharani A, Ganguly A, Bhargava KD. Salutary effect of Terminalia Arjuna in patients with severe refractory heart failure. Int J Cardiol 1995 May;49(3):191-199

Bhishagratna KL. (transl.) *Sushrut Samhita*. Varanasi, India. Chowkhambha Sanskrit Series.1991

Bone ME; Wilkinson DJ; Young JR; McNeil J; Charlton S. Ginger Root-A New Antiemetic. The Effect of Ginger Root on Postoperative Nausea and Vomiting after Major Gynaecological Surgery . Anaesthesia, 45: 8, 1990 Aug, 669-71

Dash B. *Massage Therapy in Ayurveda.*

New Delhi, India. Concept Publishing, 1992

Dwivedi S, Agarwal MP. Antianginal and cardioprotective effects of Terminalia arjuna, an indigenous drug, in coronary artery disease. J Assoc Physicians India 1994 Apr;42(4):287-289

Frawley D, Lad V. *Yoga of Herbs*. Santa Fe, NM. Lotus 109

Press. 1986 Grontved, A; Brask T, Kambskard J, Hentzer E. Ginger

Root Against Seasickness. A Controlled Trial on the Open Sea. Acta Otolaryngology (Stockh) 105: 1-2 1998. Jan-Feb 45-9

India Currents Magazine. Stressed Out? Try Sitar Music. Page 14. Dec. 1995-Jan. 1996

Itokawa H; Morita H; Takeya K. Solution

forms of an antitumor cyclic hexapeptide, RA-VII in dimethyl sulfoxide-d6 from nuclear magnetic resonance studies. Chem Pharm Bull (Tokyo), 40: 4, 1992 Apr, 1050-2

Jacob A, Pandey M, Kapoor S, Saroja R. Effect of the Indian gooseberry (amla) on serum cholesterol levels in men aged 35-55 years. Eur J Clin Nutr 1988 Nov; 42(11):939-944

Johari H. *Ancient Indian Massage*. New Delhi, India. Munshiram Manoharlal Publishers. 1988

Lad V. *Ayurveda Science of Self Healing*. Santa Fe, NM. Lotus Press. 1984

Mehrotra R; Rawat S; Kulshreshtha DK; Patnaik GK; Dhawan BN. In vitro studies on the effect of certain natural products against hepatitis B virus. Indian J Med Res,

92:1990 Apr, 133-8

Miller L, Miller B. *Ayurveda and Aromatherapy*. Twin Lakes, WI. Lotus Press, 1995

Murthy SK. (transl.) *Ashtanga Hridayam (vol. 1-3)*. Varanasi, India. Krishnadas Academy.1991, 1992, 1995

Murthy SK. (transl.) *Madhava Nidanam*. Varanasi, India. Chowkhambha Orientalia. 1993

Murthy SK. (transl.) *Shangadhar Samhita*. Varanasi, India. Chokhamba Orientalia. 1984

Nadkarni KN. *Indian Materia Medica*. Bombay, India. Popular Prakashan, 1993

Patnaik N. Garden of Life. New York, NY. Doubleday. 1993

Priyadarsini KI. Free radical reactions of

curcumin in membrane models. Free Radic Biol Med 1997;23(6):838-843

110

Qian-Cutrone J, Huang S, Trimble J, Li H, Lin PF, Alam M, Klohr SE, Kadow KF. Niruriside, a new HIV REV/RRE binding inhibitor from Phyllanthus niruri. J Nat Prod 1996 Feb;59(2):196-199

Rana BK, Singh UP, Taneja V. Antifungal activity and kinetics of inhibition by essential oil isolated from leaves of Aegle marmelos. J Ethnopharmacol 1997 Jun;57(1):29-34

Shanmugasundaram ER, Rajeswari G, Baskaran K, Rajesh KBR, Shanmugasundaram K, Kizar AB. Use of Gymnema Sylvestre Leaf Extract in the Control of Blood Glucose in Insulin-Dependent Diabetes Mellitus. *J. Ethnopharmacol* 30: 3, 1990 Oct: 281-94].

Sharma PV. *Charak Samhita*. Varanasi, India. Chaukhamba Orientalia. 1994

Sharma RK, Dash B. (transl.) *Charak Samhita*. Varanasi, India. Chowkhambha Sanskrit Series Office. 1992

Siddiqui S; Faizi S; Siddiqui BS; Ghiasuddin Constituents of Azadirachta indica: isolation and structure elucidation of a new antibacterial tetranortriterpenoid, mahmoodin, and a new protolimonoid, naheedin. J Nat Prod, 55: 3, 1992 Mar, 303-10

Srivastava KC, Mustafa T. Ginger in Rheumatism and Musculoskeletal Disorders. *Med Hypothesis* 39:4, 1992 December: 342-8

Tirtha SSS. *Ayurveda Encyclopedia*. Bayville, NY. Ayurveda Holistic Center Press. 1998

Tirtha SSS. Cost-Effective Ayurvedic Therapies for Seasonal Allergies. Research paper 1998 (unpublished)

Vaya J, Belinky PA, Aviram M. Antioxidant constituents from licorice roots: isolation, structure elucidation and antioxidative capacity toward LDL oxidation. Free Radic Biol Med 1997;23(2):302-313

Verma SP, Salamone E, Goldin B. Curcumin and genistein, plant natural products, show synergistic inhibitory effects on the growth of human breast cancer MCF-7 cells induced by estrogenic pesticides. Biochem Biophys Res Commun 1997 Apr 28;233(3):692-696

Yadav SK, Jain AK, Tripathi SN, Gupta JP. Irritable bowel syndrome: therapeutic evaluation of indigenous drugs. Indian J Med Res, 90:1989 Dec, 496-503

Meditation

Tirtha SSP. *Guru Bani: 100 Ways To Attain Peace*. Bayville, NY. Ayurveda Holisitc Center Press. 1995

Tirtha, SSP. *Yoga Vani: Instructions for the Attainment of Siddhayoga*. Bayville, NY. Ayurveda Holisitc Center Press. 1990

Jyotish (Vedic Astrology)

Frawley D. *Astrology of the Seers*. Salt Lake City, UT. Passage Press. 1990

Vedic Architecture (Vastu Shastra)

Bhat MR. *Brihat Samhita*. New Delhi, India. Moltilal Banarsidass. 1986

Dagens B. (transl.) *Mayamatma*. New

Delhi, India. Sitarm Bharita Institute of Scientific Research. 1985

Rao DM. *Hidden Treasure of Vastu Shilpa Shastra and Indian Traditions*. Bangalore, India. 1995

Reddy BN. *Glimpse of Practical Vastu*. Hyderabad, India. Virgo Publications. 1983

Feng Shui

Rossbach S. *Interior Design*. New York, NY. Penguin Books. 1987

Research

Astin J. *Why Patients Use Alternative Medicine*. JAMA Vol 279, no 19, May 20, 1998

Lazarou J, Pomeranz B, Corey P. *Incidence of Adverse Drug Reactions in Hospitalized Patients*. JAMA Vol 279, no 15, April 15, 1998.

Tompkins P. & Bird C. *Secret Life of Plants*. New York, NY. Harper Collins. 1989

Index

A

abhyanga · *See* massage
About the Author · 258
Afterword · 241
Alternative Medicine · 4
Analysis · 37
Aromatherapy · 124
Ayurveda · 6

B

Bibliography · 263

C

Case Studies · 153
    Acne · 158
    Allergies · 163
    Anemia · 161
    Arthritis · 156
    Breast cancer · 158
    Childbirth · 170
    Cholesterol · 164
    colds & flu · 154
    Diabetes · 157
    Menopause · 168
    Mental · 171
    Morning Sickness · 168
    Ovarian Cysts · 166
    Parasites · 162
    Pet Therapy · 173
    PMS · 167
    Prostate Cancer · 159
    Uterine Fibroids · 166
    Weightloss · 165
Climate and Season · 138
Color Therapy · 128

D

dosha · 27
Dosha Test · 34

E

Exercise · 111

F

Feng Shui · 149
Frequently Asked Questions · 213
    Exercise · 234
    Herbs · 224
    Meditation · 230

Nutrition · 235
Self-Realization · 236
Yoga · 232

G

Glossary · 250

H

Herbs · 52
    Acid indigestion · 56
    Acne · 56
    Adrenals · 54
    Antioxidants · 56
    Anxiety · 56
    Arteriosclerosis · 56
    Arthritis · 56
    Asthma · 56
    Athletes foot · 57
    Blood · 54
    Brain · 54
    Broken bones · 57
    Candida · 57
    Chemotherapy · 57
    Cholesterol · 57
    Circulation · 57
    Colic · 57
    Colon · 54
    Constipation · 57
    Cough/cold/flu · 57
    Depression · 57
    Diabetes · 57
    Diarrhea/dysentery · 58
    Digestion · 58
    Doses · 62
    Dysmenorrhea · 58
    Ears · 58
    Eczema · 58
    Epilepsy · 58
    Eyes · 54
    Fear · 58
    Female reproductive · 54
    Fibroids · 58
    flu · 57
    Gall stones · 58
    Gas · 58
    Heart · 54
    Hepatitis · 58
    High blood pressure · 59
    Immune system · 54
    Impatience · 59
    Impotency · 59
    Jaundice · 59
    Kidney · 54
    Kidney stones · 59
    Lethargy · 59
    Liver · 54
    Low blood pressure · 59
    Lungs · 54
    Lymph · 55
    Male reproductive · 55
    Memory · 59
    Menopause · 59
    Menorrhagia · 59
    Menstrual cramps · 59
    Mononucleosis · 60
    Morning sickness · 60
    Mouth · 55
    Muscle building · 55
    Nausea · 60
    Nerves · 55
    Pain · 60

Pancreas · 55
Parasites · 60
PMS · 60
Psoriasis · 60
Senility · 60
Skin · 55
Spleen · 55
Sprue · 60
Stress · 60
Tendons · 55
Toothache · 60
Tumors · 61
Ulcers · 61
Urinary · 61
Urinary tract infections · 61
Veins · 55
Weight · 61
Worry · 61
Yeast Infections · 61
Holistic Medicine · 4

J

Jyotish - Vedic Astrology · 141

K

Kapha · 27

M

Massage · 105
Meditation · 116
Music Therapy · 122

N

Nutrition · 65
    Mutually Contradictory Foods · 103

P

Pancha Karma · 130
Pitta · 27
prakrti · 27

S

Scientific Research · 179
    Herbs · 182
Self-Education · 257
six stages of disease development · 40
Six tastes · 30
Sleep · 113

T

Three Origin Sites of Illness · 39

V

Vastu Shastra · 147
Vata · 27

Y

Yoga · 110

Other books by the Swami Sadashiva Tirtha

Ayurveda Encyclopedia Natural Secrets For Healing, Prevention & Longevity

An exhaustive and in-depth presentation of all aspects of Ayurveda. Information available for the first time in a book published outside of India:

- 85 herb materia medica with photos
- 100-page chapter on Ayurvedic Yoga postures with illustrations
- Modern scientific research on Ayurvedic herbs
- Parallels and differences between Ayurveda and modern medicine
    - Anatomical/physiological discussions & diagrams
    - modern application of ancient practices
- Pancha karma therapies: complete discussion (traditional/Kerala styles)
- Pulse analysis determining dosha & vikriti
- 700 pages; therapies include: herbology, nutrition, exercise,

abhyañga, aromatherapy, meditation, chakra therapy, ethics, pancha karma, color therapy, music therapy, gem therapy, Ayurvedic psychology, spiritual counseling, Ayurvedic yoga postures, mantra & nada (sound therapy)
- Related topics: Jyotish (Vedic Astrology) Vastu Shastra (Vedic Architecture) Feng Shui
- Edited for accuracy and authenticity by three Ayurvedic doctors
- Hundreds of photos and diagrams including drawings of Dhanwantari, Ashwin twins, Atreya and Bharadwaja
- 30,000+ copies in print

Professional praise for the Ayurveda Encyclopedia

"...encyclopedia is exactly what this book is. The appendix is a book in itself...I took an eight-week course on Ayurveda and the course text book was not even close to being as comprehensive as the Ayurveda...you definitely need this book. The depth and mass of information available here will undoubtedly teach you something new on this ancient healing system." *Alternative Healthcare Management Magazine*

"...the most comprehensive, clear and user friendly resource book on Ayurveda available today...provides western medical translations and a valuable glossary."

Joseph Loizza, MD Director, Columbia Presbyterian Center for Meditation and Healing & Healthcare Project Director/Dharam Hinduja India Research Ctr.

Available on Amazon

Bhagavad Gita for Modern Times

In this new translation and commentary on the ancient Sanskrit text, Swami Tirtha offers a completely fresh and accessible interpretation, making it easy to apply its teachings to daily life. The timeless wisdom of the Gita is illuminated by modern-day, real-world instances examining personal spiritual goals, and family, career, social, and environmental issues germane to today's seeker of wisdom and truth.

Students of Eastern philosophy, yoga enthusiasts, parents, and entrepreneurs looking beyond *The Art of War* for inspiration will appreciate the techniques for relieving stress, discovering peace, creating self-worth, and enhancing spiritual awareness. Each page demonstrates how ancient and universal spiritual patterns can help answer common life questions and provide meaningful purpose and direction. A guide for living in a world that is often blind to what is most relevant—spirit—this explication of one of the cornerstones of spirituality will have universal, enduring appeal. Available on Amazon

Stress-Free College Student

An engaging read with easy-to-access relaxation tools to help students have a more productive study time and enjoyable social activities. Stress management tips are offered for all areas of college life—workload, finances, social life, health, emotions, and spirit/self-worth. Find quick inspiration from pertinent quotes, transformative photos, and topic-related cartoons.

Benefit from reading natural tips and success stories from students using stress-management tools. Ironically, college stress is at an all-time high, just when natural stress-management therapies have become accepted and scientifically validated. Swamiji is honored to help transform the college experience to be more manageable and enjoyable, so the next generation will have a better quality of life. Swamiji's biggest tragedy also became his greatest gift. While he doesn't wish such a tragedy on anyone, he is grateful to share with you that beautiful things can come out of your darkest days. Available on Amazon

21 Days of Joy

Enjoy this helpful hands-on guide to live more joy in your life. Since it only takes 21 days for the brain to create a new habit, this book makes it easy for you to transform and live the life of your dreams.

Twenty-one tips and cartoons to train your brain to live and think in a joyful manner.
Available on Amazon

www.ingramcontent.com/pod-product-compliance
Lightning Source LLC
LaVergne TN
LVHW051514070426
835507LV00023B/3112